"We are all—every one of 'special interests.' By prc  lobbying, *Persuading Congress* demystifies the ways in which citizens can influence legislation and achieve their public policy objectives. Anyone who wants to make a difference through legislation—not just executives—needs to read this book, master its lessons, and keep it handy."

F. Christopher Arterton
Dean, Graduate School of Political Management
The George Washington University

"This revealing book pulls back the curtain on the Congressional decision-making process and, best of all, provides invaluable advice to corporate executives on effectively influencing not just national and local legislation but the corporate environment as well."

Robert Clements
Chairman & CEO, EverBank Financial Corp.

"The Constitution gives Americans the right to petition their government for a redress of grievances. And no legislature is more accessible to its own people than the United States Congress. But rights and access alone do not translate into effective engagement or useful political action. In *Persuading Congress*, Joseph Gibson, a longtime veteran of Capitol Hill, offers masterful counsel to anyone who wants to work well with Congress. In Washington, there are well over 10,000 registered lobbyists. Very few grasp and convey the keys to successful advocacy as well as Gibson does."

Martin Gold
Covington & Burling, Washington, DC

A Practical Guide to Parlaying an Understanding
of Congressional Folkways and Dynamics
into Successful Advocacy on Capitol Hill

How to Spend
Less and Get
More from
Congress:
Candid Advice
for Executives

By Joseph Gibson

Persuading
Congress

TheCapitol.Net, Inc. is a non-partisan firm that annually provides continuing professional education and information for thousands of government and business leaders that strengthens representative government and the rule of law.

Our publications and courses, written and taught by *current* Washington insiders who are all independent subject matter experts, show how Washington works.™ Our products and services can be found on our web site at *<www.TheCapitol.Net>*.

Additional copies of *Persuading Congress* can be ordered online: *<www.PersuadingCongress.com>*.

Design and production by Zaccarine Design, Inc., Evanston, IL; 847-864-3994.

∞ The paper used in this publication exceeds the requirements of the American National Standard for Information Sciences—Permanence of Paper for Printed Library Materials, ANSI Z39.48-1992.

Copyright ©2010 By TheCapitol.Net, Inc.
            PO Box 25706
            Alexandria, VA 22313-5706
            703-739-3790 Toll free: 1-877-228-5086
            <www.TheCapitol.Net>

All Rights Reserved. Printed in the United States of America.

v 1

Persuading Congress
Softcover: ISBN: 158733-164-0   Hardbound: ISBN: 158733-173-X
            ISBN 13: 978-1-58733-164-0   ISBN 13: 978-1-58733-173-2

Dedication

*To my wife, Heath,
and my daughter, Greta,
the loves of my life.*

Table of Contents

Part II:
How You Can Influence Congress

About the Author

Joseph Gibson has worked in the legislative, executive, and judicial branches of the federal government. He has lobbied members of Congress and their staffs, advocated on behalf of the executive branch, and argued cases in federal and state courts.

He grew up in Waycross, Georgia, and then attended Yale University, where he received a bachelor's degree in political science. After graduation, he spent a year working as a staffer on the Senate Judiciary Committee. He then went to Yale Law School, where he earned his J.D. degree.

After law school, he clerked for the Hon. R. Lanier Anderson, III, of the United States Court of Appeals for the Eleventh Circuit in Macon, Georgia. He then returned to Washington where he spent the next six and a half years as a litigator with private law firms.

Although he was not particularly interested in politics at the time, the Republican takeover of Congress in 1994 led, through a series of connections and circumstances, to his getting a job as an antitrust counsel for the House Judiciary Committee under Chairman Henry Hyde of Illinois. From there, he rose to chief antitrust counsel for the committee. In 2002 he became a deputy assistant attorney general representing the legislative interests of the Department of Justice.

In 2003, he returned to the House Judiciary Committee as its chief legislative counsel and parliamentarian under Chairman Jim Sensenbrenner of Wisconsin. After two years there, he became chief of staff to Representative Lamar Smith of Texas. After the 2006 election, he became chief minority counsel of the committee. He has now returned to the private sector where he lobbies on antitrust, intellectual property, and other business issues at the law firm of Constantine Cannon LLC.

He and his wife, Heath, live in Washington and New York with their daughter. The views expressed here are entirely his own and do not necessarily represent those of any other person or group.

Preface

What happens in Congress affects all of our lives and extends into every corner of the economy. Because so much is at stake there, businesses and other interest groups spend billions of dollars each year trying to influence legislation.

Yet, most of these efforts are doomed to futility from the outset. Only a small percentage of the bills introduced in Congress actually become law, and most interested parties do not fully understand why those few bills succeed. More importantly, how to get Congress to do what they want remains a mystery to them. It is as if everyone in the place is speaking in the ancient Greek of the first democracy.

This book will help you understand Congress. Written from the perspective of one who has helped put a lot of bills on the president's desk and helped stop a lot more, this book explains in everyday terms why Congress behaves as it does. Then it shows you how you can best deploy whatever resources you have to move Congress in your direction.

You need no longer look on in wonder at what goes on in Congress. This book will allow you to read the news every day and understand what drives congressional actions. More importantly, you will no longer waste your time and money on lobbying and advocacy strategies that do not help your cause or, worse yet, actually hurt it. You will also learn when congressional actions can and cannot happen, allowing you to spend your resources elsewhere if necessary.

Because you have limited time, this book sticks to the basics and its chapters are short so that it can be digested rapidly in smaller chunks. Its advice applies to anyone who wants to affect the outcomes in Congress.[1]

---

1. For a detailed discussion of legislative procedure, see Michael L. Koempel and Judy Schneider, *Congressional Deskbook: The Practical and Comprehensive Guide to Congress* (5th ed. 2007).

Chapter 1

What You Don't Know about Congress Can Hurt Your Organization

I magine yourself as the CEO of one of America's leading banks on Monday, October 13, 2008. You have seen banks crashing around you for the last several weeks. Your bank has some troubled assets, but it has adequate capital. A week and a half ago, Congress acceded to the requests of the waning Bush administration and passed legislation to allow the government to buy up the troubled assets that caused the crisis. You are beginning to feel a bit of relief as the program kicks into action.

With no warning, you are summoned to the Treasury Department for a command performance. At the meeting, the Republican Treasury Secretary tells you that the government has changed course and will now use the money to buy stock in your bank. You are expected to take the money whether you want it or not. And, by the way, since you will be deciding "voluntarily" to take public money, you will also have to accept "voluntary" restrictions on your compensation and that of your senior executives. What was sold to you and the country as a troubled asset relief program has, in a matter of few days, become something of a bank nationalization program.

In your head, you think this cannot be right—it's a bait and switch. But you check with your lawyers and find that, much to your dismay, the language of the bill actually allows significant government control of your bank. Welcome to all kinds of new problems—not what you bargained for.

This may sound like fiction, but it happened. And if you manage any organization in the United States, something similar can happen to you. While it may not reach this scale, what happens in Congress affects your organization. Just like these highly sophisticated bankers, you may not even know what hit you until it is too late. Congress cannot only impose costs on your organization—it can change your entire way of doing business.

Organizational leaders often do not understand what happens in Congress. As a result, they frequently waste money in misguided attempts to influence its actions. Or worse yet, these leaders simply ignore Congress altogether. They do so at their peril.

Chapter 2

How to Use This Book

Before you can influence Congress, you have to understand how it works. The first part of the book, **How Congress Works** (Chapters 3–14), describes how Congress operates internally (Chapters 3–7) as well as the various external influences on it (Chapters 8–14).

This book assumes that you know the basic constitutional workings of Congress. If you do not remember them from your high school government class, Appendix A explains the congressional aspects of the Constitution in layman's language. If you feel you already know how Congress works, feel free to skip over Chapters 3–14.

The second part of the book, **How You Can Influence Congress** (Chapters 15–44), describes some fundamental facts of life in Congress, some tools you can use, some opportunities you can take advantage of in your efforts, and some long-term considerations.

This book can be read as a whole. Each chapter can also be read as a separate unit for a quick review of that topic. For that reason, some ideas are repeated in several chapters as appropriate.

Finally, this book conveys the observations, impressions, and experiences of one former congressional staffer. It provides practical guidance on the ways of Congress—it is not intended to be a comprehensive or scientific study.

For a much more detailed treatment of the legislative process, see *Congressional Deskbook*, also published by TheCapitol.Net.

Part I
How Congress Works

A. Internal Dynamics of Congress
Chapters 3–7

B. External Influences on Congress
Chapters 8–14

A. Internal Dynamics of Congress

Summary of Chapters 3–7

- Most members of Congress had comfortable lives before they ran, but they decided to give up those lives for the drudgery and constant pressure of holding a seat in Congress. Every member volunteered for that tradeoff. View all interactions with members through that prism. (*Chapter 3*)

- Party leaders are elected by the members of their caucuses, and they lead through persuasion rather than coercion. Party leaders have much more influence than rank-and-file members. Work to build relationships with them. (*Chapter 4*)

- Party leaders determine which members get on which committees and which members lead the committees for their party. Committees are where most of the detailed work on legislation is done. Committees are more important in the House than they are in the Senate because members who are not members of the relevant committees have fewer opportunities to offer floor amendments in the House. Use your limited resources to develop relationships with those members who serve on the committees that have jurisdiction over your issues. (*Chapter 5*)

- Congressional staffers have significant influence in the modern Congress. Get to know the staffers who work on your issues and educate them. (*Chapter 6*)

- Congress operates under a wide variety of rules and practices, and they can control outcomes. The House and Senate rules differ significantly. A good lobbyist should help you to understand how the rules affect your situation. (*Chapter 7*)

Chapter 3

Members of Congress

Even though they have won an election or two, members of Congress live, breathe, eat, and sleep just like the rest of us.[2] They come from all walks of life and embody many interesting individual traits and ideas. As a group, they have more than their fair share of larger-than-life characters. Some are loud; some are quiet. Some are mean-spirited; some are kindly. Some are studious; some like to party. One famous partying member even inspired a book and a movie entitled *Charlie Wilson's War* that you may have seen.

But members also share many characteristics in common. For example, most members worked in some other occupation before they came to Congress. Many practiced law, but others captained boats, treated sick people or animals, or played professional sports. A few have spent all of their adult lives as politicians, and a few never worked before running for office because of family wealth. But most members held down a real job before they ran.

In fact, most earned advanced degrees, did well in their previous careers, and held positions of influence in their local communities. Former Senator Fred Thompson's story illustrates how interesting the career paths of members can be. A successful attorney, he first came to

---

2. For convenience, this book refers to representatives and senators generically as members of Congress, or more simply members, unless there is a need to distinguish between the two. Likewise, this book refers to the areas they represent as their districts whether they are states or congressional districts.

public attention as the Republican counsel for Senator Howard Baker on the Senate Watergate Committee. When one of his legal cases became the basis for a movie, he was asked to play himself. From that first role, he built a successful acting career. In 1994, he ran for the Senate and won. After serving eight years, he decided to trade the unreality of serving in Congress for the mere fiction of a role in the television series *Law and Order.* Then he exchanged that life for the ordeal of a presidential campaign. After his unsuccessful 2008 presidential campaign, he became the host of a talk radio show.

While few members ever star in Hollywood movies, something impelled them to give up their comfortable life and run for office. From the outside, serving in Congress may look glamorous, but it involves a lot of hard and often unrewarding work.

Consider the demands members face. To keep their jobs, they must win a popularity contest every two or six years. They can lose that contest for any number of reasons that have nothing to do with their performance—just ask the Democrats who lost in 1994 or the Republicans who lost in 2008. No matter how well established they are, members' job security shifts with the political winds of the moment.

They must travel between their districts and Washington constantly. That alone would be physically taxing for most people. On top of that, many members maintain a household in both places on a government salary.

They face constituents who clamor for their attention at all hours. Those constituents expect the member to address any problem they may have—no matter how small. Whenever the member's district has a natural disaster, the member must drop the business of the moment and go there, regardless of the member's own needs. And that is on top of the numerous routine civic meetings that constituents expect members to attend. While making these rounds, the member must approach every unknown person they meet carefully for fear that they might offend a voter or a campaign contributor. Worse yet, they must worry that someone might catch them in an unguarded moment and record it. It only takes one slip for a politician to become an instant Internet phenomenon.

Members confront a press that often wants to know the details of their personal lives. The press also expects them to comment intelligently on any public issue at a moment's notice. Think about that— could you withstand constant public scrutiny of your personal life and business dealings? Could you say something intelligent about the story on page seven of your local paper this morning? Could you do it at a moment's notice when you had not previously been thinking about it? Could you defend whatever you said two years later when the situation has completely changed?

While they are in Washington, members interact constantly with other members, staff, constituents, and lobbyists. Almost everybody they meet wants something from them. They get praise all day long, but they never really know if it is offered sincerely. They get some perks like taxpayer-funded office space, staff, and travel, but none of them approaches the luxuries that executives of large corporations enjoy. In the past, they attended a lot of parties and fancy dinners, but in recent years, new ethics rules have restricted that.

Members must raise campaign money unceasingly. Aside from their own reelection campaigns, they must also raise money for other members and their party's campaign committees. As soon as one goal is met, another is upon them. The thirst is never slaked. They must spend large amounts of time either asking for money or attending fundraising events.

Until you get involved in fund-raising, you cannot grasp how much time members spend on it. Imagine working a full day from early in the morning until the early evening, including an hour or two of calling people you do not know and asking them for money. As your workday ends, you stop by a fund-raising reception for one of your friends, and then head across town to a two-hour dinner with more contributors. All the while, you must be charming to everyone and speak intelligently on the issues of the day.

Those who run for Congress choose a hard life. They must give up a year or two of their lives to do it, and they may well lose. Issues that were not even in play when they decided to run may determine the outcome. If they win, they face the many demands discussed above. Al-

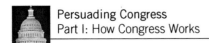

ways remember that every member of Congress made this choice at the beginning, and they make it every time they run for reelection.

Understanding that a member chose this difficult life is the first step to understanding how that member will act on your issue.[3]

---

3. Members also have many varied individual traits. If the matter you are trying to influence turns on the actions of a single member or a handful, then hire a good lobbyist who can tell you about which of their individual traits are relevant to your issue. Appendix B contains a list of tips on hiring a good lobbyist.

Chapter 4

Party Leaders

C ongress has 535 members, all of whom have ideas about what Congress should be doing. Some think we should leave the United Nations; others think we should not only stay in the United Nations, but also establish a Department of Peace. If they were left to their own devices with no structure, Congress would descend into chaos. Someone must work to resolve the conflicts and set the agenda. That job falls to party leaders.

Shortly after each congressional election, the members of each party in each chamber meet to elect their party leaders for the next Congress.[4] When the party has lost seats in the most recent election, these leadership races are often contested.[5] Sitting leaders are often challenged and occasionally defeated, but more often they will step down voluntarily if they realize they are going to lose.

Predicting the outcome of a seriously contested leadership election is notoriously difficult. It is said that the only time a candidate for a leadership position can know how a member is going to vote is when the member has looked the candidate in the eye and told the candidate that the member was going to vote for someone else. Because you will have to work with whoever emerges as the winner, you will usually benefit most by staying out of leadership elections unless you are already closely allied with one of the candidates.

---

4. Each "Congress" lasts two years. The members elected in November, 2010, will form the 112th Congress in January, 2011, and will sit until January, 2013.

5. Apart from election setbacks or scandal, leaders tend to hold on to their positions until they voluntarily step down. If there is a vacancy, leadership elections can occur in the middle of a Congress. If you are not familiar with the various leadership positions and what the jobs entail, see Appendix C.

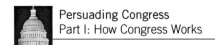
Once they are elected, the party leaders have much more power than other members, especially in the House. They determine what bills their chamber will consider, what amendments other members can offer, what the party's position will be on an issue, and how hard the party will fight for that position. They also have the ability to advance or undermine the careers of other members of their party by handing out committee assignments, committee leadership positions, campaign funds, and a variety of other benefits.

Party leaders do have certain formal powers under the rules of their chambers—most importantly, the prerogative to speak first and last on most matters if they so desire. However, most of their power is informal. They rule largely through persuasion rather than coercion. No matter how much power they may seem to have, they must always work with an eye toward maintaining the support of a majority of their caucus. But as the long-serving Speaker Sam Rayburn said: "If you want to get along, you have to go along." Members generally get ahead by going along with what their leaders want.

Since party leaders have so much more sway than other members, you should try to build long-term relationships with them. It is always a plus to have them on your side.

Chapter 5

Committees, Chairs, and Ranking Members

Both chambers of the Congress divide up their work by referring legislation to committees. Each chamber has 15 to 20 permanent committees with jurisdiction over particular subject matters. All committees are not created equal. A member who sits on the committee that writes federal tax law can raise a lot more campaign money than one who sits on a committee that oversees the Small Business Administration.

When new members arrive in Washington, they must decide what committees to try to join. They will spend most of their time working on legislation that is before their committees. Particularly in the House, members who are not on a committee have limited opportunities to influence legislation referred to that committee.

Members choose their committees for a variety of reasons. If their district consists mostly of farms, they may choose the Agriculture Committee. If a military base dominates their district, they may prefer the Armed Services Committee. If they are strongly ideological, they may join the Judiciary Committee where they can debate contentious social issues.

Each party selects a steering committee of senior members who make the decisions about which members will serve on which committees. The party leaders typically dominate these committees, and

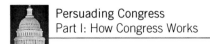
the rest of the members of the committee and the larger party conference usually rubber-stamp their decisions.

These steering committees also choose who will lead the members of the committee from their party. If their party holds the majority in that chamber, then this person becomes the chair of the committee. If their party is in the minority, this person is known as the ranking member.

Once members join a committee, they can generally remain on it as long as they serve in that chamber. However, as more senior members leave, more junior members frequently give up their assignments on less desirable committees to move up to more desirable committees.

Likewise, once a person becomes the chair or ranking member of a committee, they usually remain in that position until they serve out a term limit set by their party or step down voluntarily. However, on rare occasions, chairs or ranking members may be ousted if they do not raise enough money or do not sufficiently toe the party line. For example, in November 2008, Democrats ousted Representative John Dingell from his long tenure as their leader on the House Energy and Commerce Committee in favor of Representative Henry Waxman. Most people perceived that Representative Waxman held views closer to those of Speaker Nancy Pelosi.

An important piece of legislation generally receives a hearing and then a markup in committee before passing to the full chamber for its consideration. (A markup is a formal committee meeting to discuss and amend a piece of legislation and ultimately to vote on whether the committee will recommend its passage to the full House or Senate (see Chapter 37 and Appendix E).) The full committee or a relevant subcommittee may conduct a hearing, and the relevant subcommittee may also hold a markup before the full committee markup. The chair of the committee decides how the bill will proceed. The chair need not schedule a markup just because there has been a hearing. Likewise, the chair can schedule a markup even if there has been no hearing. Party leaders can also bring legislation before the entire chamber without any committee process at all.

Because committee markups are more important in the House, its committees tend to fight bitterly over jurisdiction. For example, after a court's antitrust consent decree broke up AT&T in 1982, the House Energy and Commerce Committee and the House Judiciary Committee struggled mightily to establish which one had jurisdiction over the future of the telecommunications industry. The Energy and Commerce Committee saw it as a communications regulatory matter. The Judiciary Committee saw it as an antitrust matter. Enormous amounts of time and energy went into to drafting bills artfully so that they would be referred to one committee or the other. To avoid this kind of fighting, it is quite common for bills that cut across jurisdictional lines to be referred to more than one committee in the House. By contrast, the Senate typically refers a bill to only one committee, and it has much less jurisdictional fighting between committees.

The members of the committee or committees that have jurisdiction over your issues are going to have the greatest ability to help you. Spend your limited time getting to know them, particularly the chair and ranking member. As Chris Matthews said in *Hardball*: "It is not who you know; it's who you get to know."

Chapter 6

Staff

C ongressional staffers do not vote or make ultimate political decisions. Nonetheless, do not make the mistake of underestimating their influence in the modern Congress.

For the first 150 or so years that Congress existed, members did most of the work themselves. As the federal government has grown, the complexity of legislation has also increased. Dealing with the details requires a level of technical expertise that no single member can possibly master. Staffers provide that expertise. In recent years, the number of staff has increased so dramatically that it now takes four large office buildings to hold the staff of the House and three for the Senate.

Each chamber employs several kinds of staff. First, every member has a personal staff that focuses on the needs of the member's district and constituents. All members get an allowance for this staff, funded by the taxpayers, based on the size of the district they represent and other factors. Then, within certain broad parameters, they may hire whomever they want to assist them so long as they do not exceed the allowance. These staffers owe their loyalty to the member who hired them, and they are expected to carry out the member's wishes.

Typically, a member will have a chief of staff, a scheduler, several legislative assistants, and a press secretary located in Washington. They will also have several caseworkers and a district director back in the district. The legislative assistants in a personal office advise the member on issues that are not within the jurisdiction of the member's committees. Usually, each member has a legislative assistant who is primarily responsible for the work of each of the member's committees.

As a general rule, Senate staffers tend to be older and more experienced than House staffers. They also tend to stick around longer because Senators serve six-year terms rather than the two-year terms of the House, giving them a little more job security. But there are many exceptions to that general rule.

In both the House and the Senate, personal office staffers tend to be younger, less experienced, and less technically knowledgeable than committee staff. However, generalization is dangerous in this area—plenty of personal office staffers have years of experience and know their issues quite well. The actual operations of members' personal office staffs vary as much as the members themselves.

Every personal office has its own personality and style. Some run smoothly; others have constant turnover. Some are easily accessible; getting into others may be like storming a castle with a moat. Some have bearskins on the wall from the member's hunting exploits; others have nothing more remarkable than a home state product like peanuts to give to visitors.

Every committee of the Congress also employs a staff. In most instances, these staff members are partisans, and they work for either the majority members of the committee or the minority members. Most substantive committee staffers have at least some plausible claim to expertise in their relevant subject matter. However, their pasts vary greatly. Some have worked the same issues for the same committee for decades; others are fresh out of school or the private sector with no government experience.

Generally, the chair of the committee hires the majority staff and the ranking member hires the minority staff. In the course of their work, committee staffers may assist all members of a committee from their party with writing speeches, drafting legislation, or a variety of other matters. However, they owe their ultimate loyalty to the member who hired them. They are expected to represent, and implement the agenda of, that member.

The party leaders also need staff to carry out their leadership duties. These staffers develop overall party positions, resolve conflicts between committees, and manage the flow of business on the floor.

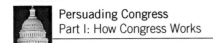
These partisan staffers represent the views of the leader who hired them and implement that leader's agenda. They tend to be the oldest and most experienced staffers. Most have served on a personal office staff, a committee staff, or both before rising to their leadership posts.[6]

When you consider what staff to approach, much depends on the nature of the issue. However, younger, less experienced personal office staff members take more risks. More experienced committee and leadership staff members have usually been burned a few times and are more cautious about new ideas. Personal office staffers will show more interest in ideas that pertain to their districts. Committee staffers will have more interest in ideas that fall within the jurisdiction of their committees. Leadership staffers look for broad, national issues that may give their parties an electoral advantage.

Staffers who work on your issue can help or hurt you a lot. Befriend and educate them.

---

6. The chambers also employ certain nonpartisan career staffers. For example, both chambers have parliamentarians who advise the leaders on procedural and jurisdictional issues. Both chambers also have lawyers who do nothing but the technical work of drafting bills. For more on legislative drafting, see Tobias Dorsey, *Legislative Drafter's Deskbook: A Practical Guide* (2006). In certain situations, these staffers can matter greatly to the outcomes, but by tradition they usually meet only with other staff and members of their chamber and only rarely with outside lobbyists.

Chapter 7

The Rules

When you listen to Congress, you may think you are hearing nothing but unorganized noise. In fact, Congress operates according to a series of internal rules that give it structure. Those rules start with the constitutional basics described in Appendix A, but they go well beyond them.

Each chamber has written rules, extensive precedents derived from those rules, and a variety of operating practices that are not written down anywhere. Each chamber has a nonpartisan parliamentarian who interprets those rules. Each party caucus and each committee has its own set of rules as well.

A complete treatment of the rules and practices would go well beyond the scope of this book.[7] What you need to know is that the rules can control the outcome of your issue. Hardly anyone understands every corner of the rules, but a good lobbyist should spot issues where the rules may control, and advise you accordingly.

Some of the most important and commonly encountered features of the rules and practices are briefly described below. We will get into these features in more detail in Part II of this book (Chapters 15–44).

First, every member of Congress represents a district. That district's interests differ from those of all other districts. When an interest particular to that district arises, that member expects to have the first shot at taking the lead on issues relating to that interest. Most other members will respect that. You will not find this congressional courtesy norm written down anywhere, but it is generally followed. For exam-

---

7. For a fuller treatment of the rules, see Chapters 8–10 of *Congressional Desk-book*.

ple, if you have a plant in Texas and you want something done for it in the Senate, go to the Texas senators first. Nothing irritates a member more than to know that you went to the senator from Louisiana first because you thought that senator would better understand your problem with the Texas plant.

Both the Senate and the House operate on a seniority system—the longer members serve, the more perks they get. They get a higher place in their committee rankings, a better pick of committee slots, better office space, and more challenging assignments from their leaders. Generally speaking, it is better to have a more senior member pushing your issue. However, you also want to make sure the member has the time to devote to it. Otherwise, you may be better off with a younger member who has less influence and more time to devote to your issue.

Committees have jurisdiction over specific subject matter areas. They want to protect those areas from encroachment by other committees. The broader their jurisdiction, the more power they have. Some issues lend themselves to solutions that might be drafted in ways that fall within the jurisdiction of more than one committee. In that case, you may want your solution drafted in a way that falls within the jurisdiction of the committee that favors your position.

For example, if you want to make mergers between airlines easier, you may want to approach the Transportation Committee because of its generally pro-industry stance. If you want to make them more difficult, you may want to approach the Judiciary Committee because of its pro-competition perspective. However, you will also want to avoid offending the prerogatives of the competing committees. A good lobbyist can advise you on the details of this in a particular situation.

In most instances, the rules of the House allow the majority to impose its will on the minority. Except for those rare instances in which the minority position attracts significant support across the aisle, the minority expects to lose most votes. Thus, the minority party frequently tries not so much to win, but to create difficult votes for the members of the majority party.

The rules limit that effort in two significant ways. First, all amendments either in committee or on the House floor must be "germane" to the underlying bill. The application of the germaneness rule can fill a tome on its own, but generally it means that the amendment must relate to the same subject matter as the underlying bill.[8]

Second, the leadership of the majority party controls what bills the House considers and what amendments members can offer. The main exception is that on most bills, the minority party gets one "motion to recommit" through which it may offer its policy alternative to the underlying bill. The minority party leadership controls the contents of this motion to recommit and they develop it in consultation with the ranking member of the committee of jurisdiction. In some cases, the majority leadership allows no amendments, and the minority party's only real chance to offer amendments to a bill is in the committee.

In the Senate, things run quite differently. First, except in very limited circumstances, the Senate does not require that amendments relate to the same subject as the underlying bill. Any senator can offer almost any amendment on any bill, whether it is relevant to that bill or not. This makes the committee markup process in the Senate much less important because senators who are not on the relevant committee can offer their amendments when the bill comes to the floor.

Second, unlike the House, the majority party leadership in the Senate does not dictate the terms of debate. Unless the leaders negotiate some other arrangement and all senators consent to it, debate and amendments are unlimited. Consideration of the bill ends only if sixty senators vote to "invoke cloture." As a practical matter, if sixty senators will not vote to cut off consideration, one senator can halt matters by threatening to engage in unlimited debate. This is known as a "filibuster," and it is limited only by the physical endurance of the senator who mounts it.[9] Former Senator Strom Thurmond once spoke on the Senate floor for twenty-four hours and eighteen minutes without a break and many years later became the oldest senator at 100 years of age.

A senator need not even make his filibuster threat publicly. The senator can simply inform his party leadership of his intentions. This is

---

8. See § 8.120 of *Congressional Deskbook*.
9. See § 8.210 of *Congressional Deskbook*.

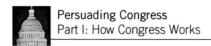
known as "putting a hold" on the bill. Except for the most important issues, a senator's putting a hold on a bill usually suffices to kill it. Because of this cumbersome system, the majority leader will only spend the precious resource of Senate floor time on important bills or those that can pass with little controversy. However, senators often release their holds after receiving some concession in a negotiation—this happens more frequently as a Congress comes to a close.

These important features of the rules only scratch the surface. We will discuss other aspects of the rules in Chapters 15–44 of this book, but this chapter gives you a basic outline of how Congress operates.

B. External Influences on Congress

Summary of Chapters 8–14

- The President is the single most powerful external influence on the actions of Congress, and he has a wide variety of ways to get Congress to follow his direction. The president's support will almost always help your cause. (*Chapter 8*)

- Federal departments differ from independent federal agencies because the departments are more directly under the president's control. Departments and agencies interact constantly with Congress in both formal and informal ways. Use that interaction to put your issues in play. (*Chapter 9*)

- The federal courts play a passive, but powerful role in putting issues before Congress. They can ignite issues or provide an excuse for Congress not to act. (*Chapter 10*)

- Through their role as filter, the news media influence what subjects the public is thinking about. They can put previously unknown issues in play. They can restrain bad behavior in members and staff. Use the news media to put your issues in play, but remember that they will pursue their own interest. (*Chapter 11*)

- Washington has so many lobbyists because so much is at stake there. Their numbers do not necessarily mean that the place is rife with corruption. Lobbyists rightly influence the actions of Congress by exercising the constitutional right to petition the government. Get the best representation in Washington that you can afford. (*Chapter 12*)

- Congress follows public opinion religiously. It is a strong force when it can be activated, but those instances are rare. Use your own voice and those of your allies to convince members what the public thinks. (*Chapter 13*)

- Members and staff are intensely focused on the next election at all times because it greatly affects their quality of life. View all issues in light of the next election and act accordingly. (*Chapter 14*)

Chapter 8

The President

The president influences Congress far more than any other outside person primarily because of the veto. So long as one-third of either chamber supports the president's position, a veto kills any bill. Congress rarely musters the votes to override one. As a result, the president holds about a third of the cards in any legislative negotiation. That third does not always control the outcome, but it is a much stronger hand than any other single player has.

Even in periods of unpopularity, the president affects Congress's ability to enact legislation. For example, after Republicans lost their majorities in Congress in the 2006 election, President Bush used the veto, or the threat of it, often during 2007 and 2008 to stymie or slow much of the congressional Democrats' agenda. The mere threat of a veto often suffices to shape legislation in the president's preferred direction. For that reason, presidents threaten vetoes much more often than they actually use them.

But the president's tools extend well beyond the veto. He can command public attention for his agenda in a way that no other single actor can. When he speaks, the press will cover his words no matter what he says. If he wants to direct the public's attention to a particular issue, he can usually do so. If he wants legislation passed, he may transmit a proposed bill to Congress and call for its enactment.

The president ultimately controls the executive departments and, to a lesser extent, the independent agencies through his appointment power. Many of these departments and agencies, acting under the president's direction, decide important policy issues including how to interpret statutes, what enforcement cases to bring, or what new rules to

promulgate. For example, on January 22, 2009, just after his inauguration, President Obama issued an executive order directing several agencies to begin the process of closing the Guantanamo Bay prison, thereby reversing President Bush's policy. Executive Order 13492 (Review and Disposition of Individuals Detained at the Guantánamo Bay Naval Base and Closure of Detention Facilities) (January 22, 2009). In early 2010, the Guantanamo prison remains open, and it continues to stir controversy. Congress, through its oversight powers, follows many of these decisions with keen interest.

Finally, it is said that the president proposes and the Congress disposes, but the president nonetheless has a great deal of say over how the federal government spends money. Under the Constitution (Article I, section 9, clause 7), Congress exercises the ultimate power of the purse. However, the president, in consultation with the departments and agencies, develops an annual budget request for the spending of the federal government every year. While Congress makes many changes to the president's budget request, that request still forms the broad outline of how money gets spent. Congress generally follows it while changing some of the details.

The president's popularity waxes and wanes, but he is always a major player in the affairs of Congress. If you are pushing an issue in Congress and the president has an interest in it, it is generally better to have him on your side.

Chapter 9

The Departments and Agencies

The vast expanse of the federal government consists of two main types of organizations: executive departments and independent agencies. Members of the president's cabinet, who report directly to him and serve at his pleasure, head the executive departments. They implement the president's agenda and carry out his policies. They cannot take a position on legislation without the approval of the White House.

Nonetheless, executive departments often have interests that go beyond the president's. In those cases, departments may subtly push positions without the president's approval. Departments often accomplish this by offering "technical assistance" to Congress. The exact parameters of that phrase are vague, but it allows the departments a certain amount of leeway on these types of issues.

Independent agencies, like the Securities and Exchange Commission or the Federal Trade Commission, typically consist of multi-member boards. The members often serve for a fixed term rather than at the pleasure of the president. Usually, the statute that creates the agency effectively requires that a majority of the board must come from the president's party and a minority from the other party. The members of these agencies need not follow the president's direction and they may take positions on legislation that differ from the president's. As a practical matter, however, the members of such an agency from the president's party generally follow his lead on policy because they received their appointment from him.

Executive departments and independent agencies (hereafter re-ferred to collectively as "agencies") generally maintain close working relationships with the members and staff of the congressional com-mittees that oversee them, and they interact constantly. This interac-tion takes place in many ways and over a wide range of issues, includ-ing phone calls, informal briefings, formal written requests for information, comments on proposed legislation, wrangling over the Senate's confirmation of agency nominees, and congressional hearings on the agency's performance or its budget.

To facilitate this communication, most agencies have a full-time staff whose principal job is to interact with Congress on behalf of the agency. These staffers are typically known as congressional liaisons. Their numbers vary depending on the size of the agency. Often a large agency will have congressional liaisons for particular components within the agency as well as a separate staff tending to the overall in-terests of the agency. These staffs usually consist of a mix of political appointees and career civil servants. In most agencies, there will be at least one political appointee leading the staff. They can work to edu-cate Congress, but cannot urge third parties to support their positions or to contact Congress on their behalf. If you want to work with an agency on a congressional issue, they are usually the best place to start.

As part of this process, an agency may request that Congress enact legislation or Congress may request the views of an agency on a pro-posed law. Occasionally, both sides may see the need for legislation as a result of their interaction or as a result of some external event. For example, after the 9/11 terrorist attacks, Congress and the executive branch came together to enact a number of measures designed to en-hance our ability to counter terrorism. If members do not have a per-sonal interest in a piece of legislation and an agency does, many mem-bers may defer to an agency's views on it, particularly when it is highly technical in nature.

With respect to an agency's performance, Congress exercises what is known as its "oversight" power—that is, it checks up on the agency to see whether it is accomplishing its mission, correctly enforcing or administering the law, and wisely spending its money. This process can take many forms, but all of them add up to an ongoing conversation between the Congress and the agency about the agency's work. It can be friendly, neutral, or adversarial, and it can be all of these at different hours of any given day.

During budget season, even more oversight occurs. Congress passes annual appropriations bills to fund the agencies. Thus, members of the appropriations committees have extensive influence over how agencies conduct their business. They have all sorts of questions for agencies. The agencies must respond to them or they may risk losing part of their budgets.

The oversight process goes on all the time. It offers fertile ground for putting issues into play. One congressional staffer asking a question to an agency can ignite an issue. Contrast that with the immense difficulty of passing legislation. Much depends on the exact nature of your problem, but if you want to get the attention of someone in an agency, use the tools and opportunities that congressional oversight provides.

Chapter 10

The Courts

In Federalist Paper No. 78, Alexander Hamilton referred to the federal courts as the "weakest branch" of the new federal government. In modern times that is, at a minimum, a proposition subject to debate.

On the one hand, the federal courts cannot initiate action. They may only decide the cases that litigants bring to them and that fall within their jurisdiction. Congress defines their jurisdiction by statute and, by comparison with most state courts, federal courts have relatively limited jurisdiction.

On the other hand, however, the Supreme Court and the lower federal courts have dramatically increased their influence in American life, beginning with the decisions of the Warren Court in the 1950s and 1960s. They now decide any number of issues that once resided solely in the political arena. The reasons for that change and its desirability would fill another book. But for purposes of this book, you need to know that federal court decisions now affect Congress in significant ways.

Aside from matters pertaining to the federal courts' administration, the federal judiciary has little direct influence on an issue once it is before Congress. Federal judges do not lobby Congress or express their views on legislation in most circumstances.

However, the federal courts greatly influence what issues are put in play. Consider the Supreme Court's decisions in *Brown v. Board of Education*, 347 U.S. 483 (1954) and *Roe v. Wade*, 410 U.S. 113 (1973). These cases and others like them set off years of struggle within the Congress. Likewise, it is not uncommon for a federal court's decision to put some lesser issue of statutory interpretation in play. Congress frequently passes a "fix" bill when it feels that a federal court has misinterpreted its work. For example, the first bill that President Obama signed, the Lilly Ledbetter Fair Pay Act of 2009, Pub. L. No. 111-2, 123 Stat. 5 (2009), overturned a Supreme Court decision that Congress felt misinterpreted the statute of limitations for a sex discrimination law. *Ledbetter v. Goodyear Tire & Rubber Co.*, 550 U.S. 618 (2007).

Federal courts can also serve as an excuse for congressional inaction. Members who favor inaction may point to a pending court case on the same issue and argue that Congress should await the court's decision before acting.

Finally, the federal courts sometimes resolve disputes between members of Congress (the litigation between Representative Boehner and Representative McDermott over the release of a surreptitiously taped 1996 phone conversation); between the executive and legislative branches (the litigation over the Justice Department's 2006 search of Representative Jefferson's congressional office, or the House Judiciary Committee subpoenas of Bush White House aides issued in 2007); or between other parties that may have a profound impact on Congress (the litigation resolving the disputed 2000 presidential election). In all these ways, courts can significantly affect Congress, but they do not initiate that influence. They decide what litigants bring to them.

For all these reasons, Congress watches the decisions of the federal courts closely and members may sometimes even file "friend of the court" briefs in appropriate cases. Like it or not, the federal courts may play a role in your issue. Unless you are a party in the case, you may have little chance to influence a court's decision. But you should be aware that Congress may be watching the decision and preparing to act or not act because of it.

Chapter 11

The News Media

Mombers of Congress and reporters need each other. Members need reporters to communicate information to the public. Reporters need members to say and do interesting things to fill the oceans of empty space they face each day. In any one-on-one relationship between a member and a reporter, each person can help or hurt the other. Usually, both parties do some of both.

Most of us rarely, if ever, interact with the news media, and so we may find it hard to imagine the daily experience of public figures. As a member of Congress, you face daily, persistent questioning on every conceivable subject, including your personal life. Not only that, your job depends on giving answers that you can defend today and in the future. Any slip can provoke an immediate firestorm or come back to bite you years later, long after you have forgotten what you said. In the age of ever-present hand-held video cameras, it takes only seconds for a few ill-chosen words to travel around the Internet.

Recall the unfortunate saga of Senator George Allen of Virginia. In 2006, he was coasting to reelection and on track to run a strong presidential campaign in 2008 until, in an unguarded moment, he referred to a heckler as a "macaca"—a term previously unknown to most of the public. It was all downhill from there: he lost his reelection bid and left politics.

When Congress is in session, a tremendous amount of activity goes on each day. The news media choose a small portion of that activity to relay back to their audience. Through that winnowing process, they shape public opinion. With the advent of the Internet, email, blogging, C-SPAN, Facebook, and Twitter, a dedicated citizen can learn a lot about Congress. Another potent news source is talk radio: some have credited it with igniting the firestorm of controversy over health care reform that broke out in town hall meetings in August, 2009. These new communications tools certainly give members new ways to reach the public over the heads of the traditional news media.

But the reality is that relatively few people have the time or interest to follow the details of congressional activity closely in these new ways. The situation is constantly evolving, but most people still find out whatever they know about Congress through what they hear, see, or read in the traditional news media.

Through the stories they write, reporters affect congressional action. They uncover previously unknown issues and bring them to public attention. A good example was the substandard living conditions for soldiers going through outpatient treatment at Walter Reed Army Medical Center in 2007. When *The Washington Post* reported that story on February 18, 2007, Congress swung into action. But for the story, the conditions would likely have remained a hidden scandal.

More broadly, the news media largely determine what topics within the realm of current events that the public thinks about. If people think about Congress at all, they tend to think about whatever issue they hear about in the news regardless of whether it otherwise interests them. Pundits tend to comment on the same topics. The press itself tends to have a pack mentality. Once it begins to focus on a particular issue, other issues get less attention. All of these tendencies reinforce the others.

Consider the cases of Elian Gonzalez and Terri Schiavo. You may recall that Gonzalez was a young Cuban boy who escaped to the United States with his mother in November 1999. His mother died on the trip. After a protracted controversy, he was returned to his father in Cuba. Although Congress never acted on the case, members took a variety of actions to try to influence its progress including introducing private bills to adjust his immigration status. See H.R. 3532 and S. 2314 in the 106th Congress (1999–2000).

Schiavo was a young Florida woman who was in a persistent vegetative state as a result of a sudden collapse. Her husband sought to have her feeding tube removed over the objections of her parents and he ultimately succeeded after a long legal battle. In early 2005, after the parents' state court appeals were exhausted, Congress rushed back from its Easter recess and passed a special bill that afforded the parents a hearing in federal court. Pub. L. No. 109-3, 119 Stat. 15 (2005).

When the news media focused intensely on these cases, every American held an opinion about them. At the same time, Congress followed them passionately. When the stories faded from the news, Congress and the public lost interest.

Another function of the news media is to restrain bad behavior. Because members and their staffs fear public exposure, all manner of mischief does not happen. Inducing this fear greatly serves the public interest. Unfortunately, this relentless public scrutiny may also discourage highly qualified people from running for Congress at all.

Depending on your circumstances, reporters can help you by highlighting your issue or restraining action that you do not want. However, when you work with reporters, you should always keep in mind that— just like everyone else in the world—they pursue their self-interest, not yours. If the two interests happen to coincide, you will enjoy the relationship. But remember that interests can coincide for a time and then diverge. Having set those forces loose, you cannot control their direction, intensity, or duration. Before enlisting the news media as an ally, always think long and hard about the consequences.

Many large firms employ public relations professionals to help them navigate their relations with the news media. That is money well spent for a large public company. If you are not that big, many independent firms offer public relations services. They can tailor their services and prices to your needs—if you need them. If your issue does not attract great public interest, you can probably get along without them. However, you should get public relations help if you find yourself in any highly publicized congressional investigation. In that situation, press demands can overwhelm you and public relations professionals can help you fend them off.[10]

---

10. For a good overview of media relations and how they work in Washington, see Brad Fitch, *Media Relations Handbook* (2004).

Chapter 12

Interest Groups and Lobbyists

Washington teems with thousands of lobbyists, interest groups, and think tanks—all trying to affect public policy. Many people find this unseemly. But the lobbyists are there for a reason. The people paying them do not like to throw money away. Rather, the federal government reaches into an enormous number of spheres. Every day, it affects the lives and livelihoods of millions of people.

Intelligent people naturally want an advocate before this behemoth. So long as the government remains at anything approaching its current size, this situation will continue. As the government grows further, the number of lobbyists and interest groups will continue to increase.

The First Amendment of the Constitution protects all of this activity. It says: "Congress shall make no law … abridging … the right of the people … to petition the Government for a redress of grievances." Lobbyists and interest groups petition the government for a living. Unbeknownst to you, dozens of lobbyists you have never met represent your interests in one form or another—or at least they purport to do so.

Many people survey the scene and conclude that it all must be corrupt. To be sure, corruption occurs in Washington. In recent years, the news media have rightly reported the tawdry details of some celebrated cases. That is fine—that is their job. But if that is all you hear about Washington, you may believe that is all that goes on there. In fact, the vast majority of lobbyists, members, and staff conduct their daily business honestly. They have too much to lose by not doing so. If you do not believe that, contact former Representative Duke Cunningham or former lobbyist Jack Abramoff and ask them whether they would like to go back to where they were before their criminal acts.[11]

Aside from all that, do lobbyists and interest groups actually have any influence on Congress? The answer is yes. Of course they do. That is as it should be. Consider, for example, business issues. No member can possibly know about every aspect of one business—much less the many businesses that have interests before Congress. Members need lobbyists to explain how businesses operate before forming an opinion on their issues. Many times, these businesses will be the member's constituents, and the member will be hearing about the interests of the very people that the member represents. Just as in the courts of law, the process benefits from good advocacy on all sides of the question.

Lobbyists come in all shapes and sizes. Most large businesses employ in-house lobbyists in their Washington offices. Frequently, they also belong to numerous trade associations and informal coalitions that represent them in concert with other companies that share similar interests. Smaller businesses are less likely to have their own in-house lobbyists, but a number of trade associations represent them. Literally thousands of trade associations have offices in Washington. They run the gamut from the most general, like the Chamber of Commerce, to those that represent one particular industry, like the National Association of Convenience Stores, to those that represent even narrower slices of an industry.

Beyond that, many independent law firms and lobbying firms offer their government relations services for a fee. Most companies and trade associations have some of these independent lobbying firms on retainer. The nature of the representation varies depending on the circumstances. Sometimes, these lobbyists are hired on a short-term, one-project basis. Others are hired on a long-term, continuing basis to handle whatever issues may arise. Likewise, in some cases, they are

---

11. For a discussion of ethics in lobbying, see Chapter 2 of Deanna Gelak, *Lobbying and Advocacy* (2008).

hired to engage in active advocacy; in other cases, they are hired simply to monitor an issue and provide periodic updates.

But that brief description covers only the world of for-profit lobbyists. Hundreds of other groups operate in Washington to push Congress to do whatever they perceive serves the public interest. These groups may be broad or narrow. They may be powerful or weak. We need not get into them in detail here, but you should know that they are players in the debate. Members and staff often perceive them to have a public-spirited disinterestedness that others do not have. For that reason, they can help you if your interests coincide with theirs. They can also hurt your cause if they oppose you and members perceive them as advocates for the public interest while you are an advocate solely for your interest.

Washington is also full of think tanks that employ scholars to comment on public policy. These groups rarely lobby directly. However, for long-term policy debates, they can help refine ideas and get them into the debate.

If you run an organization, you need representation in Washington. You can safely bet that the other organizations in your sphere have representatives who are busily working in Washington to give their clients an advantage. However, how much representation you need depends on your size. If you are a small organization, a trade association may adequately represent your interests and it may be all you can afford. While that may not be a perfect option, it beats going unrepresented. As you get larger, you might consider hiring an outside lobbyist, establishing a Washington office, or both. If you are in a highly regulated industry or one that is likely to become highly regulated in the foreseeable future, you need Washington representation even more than you would otherwise.

Many up-and-coming businesses want to keep themselves free from the tumult of Congress. That works for a while, but if you earn a pile of cash, Congress will focus on you. Microsoft learned that in the 1990s, and Google learned it in the 2000s. The sooner you get involved, the sooner you can protect and advocate your interests.

Chapter 13

The Public and Public Opinion

C ontrary to popular belief, Congress follows public opinion with religious fervor. Many misguided policies flow from that. But Congress also tries to influence public opinion. Politics is mostly about talk, and much of the daily conversation in Congress seeks to win over public opinion.

If you are trying to drive Congress's actions, public opinion can be an incredibly strong force. You cannot control it, but you can sometimes shape it and use it to your advantage. When it supports you, you can ride it to favorable results. When it opposes you, you can be wiped out regardless of the merits of your arguments.

Members also respond to individual members of the public. If you do not believe this, write a letter or an email to your member and ask a question. You will get a response. You may feel it is canned, but you will get a response.

Use this to your advantage. You have a voice and your member of Congress has to listen to it. Members generally give first priority to those who live in their district. If you are talking to your member, make sure to mention that you live in the district. If you are talking to another member, try to enlist the support of someone from the member's district who shares your interest. You would be surprised at how many people overlook the simple power of constituents talking to members.

Because of the effects of public opinion on what Congress does, you should always think through the public opinion aspect of your problem. Many times, the public simply will have no interest in your problem. In other cases, the public or the news media will already have an interest and you will have to decide how to act within that pre-existing interest. Sometimes the public and the news media do not have a pre-existing interest, but you can generate an interest that helps you. In that kind of case, you should not let this tool go unused.[12]

---

12. For more information about how to use the media, see *Media Relations Handbook*.

Chapter 14

Elections

Most members and staffers spend a good part of every day thinking about how their official actions may affect the next election. The election determines matters of great import for them: whether they will have a job, and whether their party will control their chamber. That, in turn, determines whether they can enact their agenda and satisfy their ambitions. If they win, their life gets better. If they lose, their life gets worse. It is as simple as that. For all those reasons, they focus on the next election intensely and it affects everything they do.

Until you experience it, you cannot appreciate how all-consuming it is. You absolutely must think about how your issue affects the next election. Nothing can bring you to victory or defeat more quickly. If members and their staffs believe that taking your side helps them win the election, they will welcome you like a king. If they believe that it will cause them to lose the next election, they will shun you.

That being said, most issues will have no effect on the next election. When that is the case, then you can safely return to policy arguments to justify your position.

However, you also have to get space on the agenda of a committee or a chamber. Issues that affect the next election usually get first priority and they crowd out many others. In fact, very few of the bills introduced in any given Congress actually make it into law. Most die simply because they are not compelling enough to force their way on to the overpacked agenda. If you are trying to kill a bill, this factor works for you. If you are trying to get a bill passed, it works against you unless your bill affects that election.

Elections matter to members and staffers. Their jobs depend on the results of the next election, and therefore it is always the most important election of all time to them. You cannot succeed unless you view everything through that lens.

Part II
How You Can Influence Congress

A. Facts of Life

Summary of Chapters 15–20

- In the United States Congress, self-interest rules. It makes the process understandable and easier to influence. Put your requests to members in terms of their self-interest if possible. (*Chapter 15*)

- Bashful people do not run for Congress. Members have egos. Appeal to that ego and work within the member's view of the world if you want to influence that member. (*Chapter 16*)

- Members come to Congress with an ideology. Representatives generally have more freedom to hold extreme views because they represent smaller constituencies than senators. Always take a member's ideology into account in a pitch to them. Do not waste time on members who are not "gettable" because of their ideology or party affiliation. Look for members who may have a district interest that may require them to vote against their ideology or party affiliation. (*Chapter 17*)

- Members want credit for what they do because when they run for reelection, they need to point to accomplishments. Include within your pitches the opportunities that a member will have to take credit for the desired action and show the member how it will happen. (*Chapter 18*)

- Congress is subject to inertia. It is much easier for Congress not to act than to change the status quo. Consider this carefully before approaching Congress for a solution to your problem. It usually takes a long time to get a law passed. If time is short, you may want to consider other options. (*Chapter 19*)

- The size of the majority matters in both chambers. If it is small, a few members in the middle have disproportionate power. If it is large, party leaders may more easily impose their will. Focus your efforts on those who hold the power in each situation. (*Chapter 20*)

Chapter 15

Self-Interest

I f you learn nothing else from this book, remember this: in Congress, self-interest rules. All parties want to further their self-interest and they act accordingly. The same is true in your environment. However, you have to experience it to believe how relentless it is in Congress.

Do not be put off by this. Self-interest is not necessarily a bad thing. For one thing, the framers of the Constitution grasped this utterly human tendency all too well. They carefully designed the system to pit interest against interest so that no one got too much power. They built in checks and balances at every turn.

In addition, knowing this makes the process entirely understandable—if not transparent. If you have ever been involved in litigation, a judge's reasons for deciding a case in a particular way may have puzzled you. In that process, you could not find out the reasons. In Congress, the self-interest of the players usually explains their actions. To paraphrase the famous Watergate axiom: if you want to unravel the mystery, follow the self-interest.

This aspect of Congress also provides you with powerful tools to get what you want. If you want a member (or anybody else for that matter) to do something, think about the issue from their point of view. Then try to cast whatever you want as being in that member's self-interest. Or alternatively, try to find a solution to your problem that fits with that member's self-interest. Any time you ask a member to do something, try to align the desired action with the member's self-interest. The member and the staff will assuredly think about whether it fits into their self-interest.

Almost every lobbying pitch I ever heard (and there were literally hundreds of them) went something like this: "Congressman, we would like you to do x because it would really help us if you would do x." Rarely, if ever, did I hear a pitch along the line of: "Congressman, if you did x, it would help you because of y, and by the way, it just so happens that it would solve our problem as well." Imagine yourself in the place of the member and think about which approach would more likely move you. Not all issues lend themselves to this type of appeal, but many do. In that case, you are selling yourself short if you do not make it.

Chapter 16

Ego

L et's face it: bashful people do not run for Congress. To decide to do what it takes to become a member, a person must have an ego. That is all well and good. In the congressional slugfest of competing interests, you do not want a shrinking violet as your representative.

By the same token, you have to keep ego in mind when you approach a member of Congress. They have quirks. They may see the facts of your situation quite differently from the way you do. They like to see their name mentioned positively in the newspaper and on television.

Again, knowing this gives you powerful tools to use in persuading a member to do what you want. If a member has already helped you in some way, always bring it up when you see the member and say thank you. If a member introduces a bill on your behalf, you should talk about the member's bill and the member's work on it even if you drafted it and the member has never read it. If you do not have something along this line to work with, find something else that the member has done that you like and talk about that.

Sometimes, members may make odd requests or ask questions that you find strange. You may not understand why, but always respond in some fashion. They do not like to be ignored. More importantly, they may have asked because they want to help you in a way that they cannot tell you about at the moment.

Do not schedule meetings with members unless you have a good reason to do so. When you do, respect their time. They accurately see themselves as busy people pulled in a dozen different directions every day. If you have an appointment with a member, be on time. Adapt your schedule to meet theirs. They may have to leave early because of a floor vote or a sudden realization that the local Jaycees are in town and want the member at their lunch. Realize that their schedules are always hopelessly full of conflicts and this has nothing to do with you. When you have their ear, do not abuse it. Tell them what you have to say as quickly as you reasonably can and let them go. If you get the answer that you want, stop talking and leave before it changes.

As best you can, work with members within their particular view of the world. You will not get far by trying to impose your view of the world on them. To the extent that they tell you how they see your problem, try to fit the action you seek within the range of what they view as acceptable action. This is not always possible, but it is always worth a try.

Chapter 17

Ideology

Most members of Congress decide to run for Congress the first time in part because of their ideology. They hold some beliefs that they would like to pursue in the arena of public policy-making. Some are conservative; some are liberal; and some invent their own special brands that defy conventional categories. Some adhere to their ideologies rigidly; some retreat to them when they know little about an issue; and some feel free to deviate from them whenever the mood strikes.

A good lobbyist can advise you on the ideology of any member whom you may need to approach. As a general rule, House members tend to have the freedom to hold less centrist ideological views because the constituencies they represent are smaller, more concentrated, and more homogenous. By the same token, senators tend to have less freedom to deviate from the center because they represent larger, less concentrated, and less homogenous constituencies.

For the same reasons, a primary challenger who will argue that the member is not ideologically pure enough may threaten a House member much more than a potential general election opponent. For example, in the 2008 election cycle, Democratic Representative Al Wynn and Republican Representative Chris Cannon lost primary challenges on ideological grounds even though many viewed them as generally in the mainstream of their parties. Because the primary electorate is much narrower than the overall electorate, the threat of such a challenge may require the House member to adhere to positions that others would consider extreme. Such challenges do occasionally occur in the Senate, but they are rare. For example, the threat of such a challenge caused Senator Arlen Specter to change parties in early 2009. However, in general, senators are much more likely to fear a challenge from a strong general election candidate from the other party.

Whatever a member's ideology, you should take it into account when trying to persuade them of your point of view. Doing so will help you allocate your limited resources to those who are "gettable" for your position. You should not waste your time trying to persuade members whose ideology precludes them from ever adopting your position.

Considering a member's ideology will also help you tailor your pitch in a way that will appeal to that member. You do not need to use the same pitch on every member. Some arguments work better with liberals, and some work better with conservatives. Adjust your pitch to the individual.

Party affiliation also enters into the mix here. American political parties are broad coalitions that do not adhere to one ideological line. While it is true that Democrats are usually liberal and Republicans are usually conservative, neither is necessarily so when you are dealing with an individual member of Congress. However, party affiliation indicates how most members will vote on most questions.

On certain votes, like procedural motions, party affiliation controls. Members rarely vote against their party on a procedural vote. On certain substantive votes, party leaders may let members of their own party know that the outcome of the vote affects the party's fortunes so much that the leaders expect their members to vote a certain way. On these types of votes, you may not be able to overcome the member's need to vote with the party.

Occasionally, you may show the member that voting the other way will affect the member's next election and get the member to vote against the member's party. If an issue is of great importance to the member's district, the member's party leaders may give the member a pass, or the member may simply vote against the party line without a pass. For example, in December 2008, House Republican leaders opposed, and urged other Republicans to oppose, a bailout for the automobile companies. But Michigan Republicans worked against their party's position because of the importance of the industry to their state. If your issue is susceptible to this sort of appeal, use it.

Chapter 18

Credit

Members of Congress like to get credit for what they do. They believe their jobs depend on it because their constituents are watching. When they campaign for reelection, they need to point to something and say, "I did this for you." In fact, some have even posited that politicians take only two actions: they either point with pride or view with alarm.

Seeking credit makes a lot of sense. If the people of a district sent you to Washington to represent them and then you had to face them and ask for their votes, you would want to demonstrate that you accomplished something. You would not want to stand by silently while your opponent attacked your lack of a record.

If possible, sell your idea to a member as something that the member can take credit for back home. If the member does whatever you want, make sure they get lots of credit. For example, publicize the member's favorable action in your newsletter. Let the local paper know about it. Ask the member for some other way that you can get the word out. If you succeed, let the member know that you did it. Show the member the newsletter or the local paper. Tell the member how many people saw it.

The news does not have to be anything earth-shaking, and the audience does not have to be big. Remember that members are engaged in the business of winning popularity contests one vote at a time. Any favorable press—no matter how small—helps.

It has often been said that there is no limit to what can be accomplished if no one cares who gets the credit. Perhaps that is why so little happens in Washington—members care who gets the credit for good things and the blame for bad things.

Chapter 19

Inertia

The Founders designed Congress to fail to pass laws most of the time. They feared that Congress would pass bad laws much more than they feared that it would not pass good laws. In 1787, no one imagined that the body of federal statutes would grow to what it is today. But the difficult work of enacting all those laws took Congress a long time.

Now that we have them, Congress finds it hard to repeal any of them. It is much easier—and generally speaking less risky as well—to let whatever is in place continue than it is to change anything. As a result, Congress definitely adheres to Newton's first law of motion: it tends to stay at rest unless acted on by an outside force.

If you like the status quo, this is good for you. It is easy to delay things. But if you are seeking change, you face a difficult task. It is hard to pass a law even if it is uncontroversial. It takes time. If there is controversy, then that just makes it all the harder and more time-consuming.

The point here is that you should think your problem through carefully before you approach Congress to pass a law. If you need a solution in a short time frame, think seriously about whether it is realistic to believe that Congress will actually pass a law in whatever time you have. In the right circumstances, Congress can enact laws quickly, but that is the exception, not the rule.

If the time frame is not realistic, do not spend your time seeking passage of a new law. However, think about whether Congress could do other things to solve your problem. For example, can Congress bring pressure on some agency to change its position? Can it hold a hearing that will bring public pressure on your opponents? A good lobbyist can tell you where best to direct your efforts or whether it is a waste of time to even approach Congress.

Difficult as it is, you can overcome inertia, particularly if you have a longer time frame. Many complex and controversial bills would clearly serve the public interest if enacted. However, they may take several Congresses to pass. If you have the time, do not give up simply because your bill does not pass in the current Congress or the next one. That which seems impossible at the beginning can evolve into something that everyone believes must happen in a year or two.

Inertia is a fact of life in Congress. How you can best address it depends on how much time you have to deal with your problem.

Chapter 20

Size of Majority

E very even-numbered year, voters decide the partisan makeup of the Congress that will sit for the next two years. In each chamber, one party holds the majority and the other labors in the minority. But the story only begins there. The size of the majority matters as well.

In the House, the rules dictate that the majority party's will usually prevails. Notwithstanding that, an eighty-vote margin over the minority party gives the Speaker much more freedom than a ten-vote margin does. For much of the period between 1995 and 2006, the Republicans controlled the House with narrow margins. When any close vote approached, the few moderate Republican members held disproportionate power. They could individually threaten to vote against the party line and extract concessions from their leaders. This threat gave them the power to shape legislation before it ever came to a vote.

Contrast that with the situation of Speaker Nancy Pelosi after the 2008 elections. She enjoyed roughly an eighty-vote margin. She had many moderate members in her party. Because of the size of the margin, however, they were unable to individually exercise the same power that moderate Republicans did in the prior years. They only had that power if they stuck together as a group and made their demands collectively—a hard trick to pull off. The efforts of the moderate Blue Dog Democrat faction in the summer and fall of 2009 on the health care bills are good examples of this principle at play.

In the Senate, the situation is similar. During the years of Republican control and the Democratic control in 2007–2008, the margin was always slim. The Republicans actually lost their one-vote margin in 2001–2002 because Senator James Jeffords decided to leave the party and caucus with the Democrats. When the Senate Majority Leader has a slim margin, every senator can threaten a filibuster on any matter to get concessions. The Majority Leader can never break the filibuster unless a bill has broad bipartisan support.

In 2009, however, Majority Leader Harry Reid for a time had 60 Democratic senators—enough to overcome any filibuster if all Democrats vote with him. That creates a different dynamic. Republicans could only mount a filibuster if their party united completely and they got at least one Democrat to join them. Any one or two senators could undermine the Republican position. By the same token, the January 2010 election of Senator Scott Brown as the 41st Republican completely changed the dynamic again in the Senate. In either case, Senator Reid still cannot impose his will in the way that Speaker Pelosi can, but he needs to make many fewer concessions to get things done in 2009–2010 than he did during 2007–2008.

When margins are slim, individual members, particularly the centrist ones, have greater power to make demands on their leaders in return for their votes. When margins are wider, party leaders have a greater ability to impose their will without change. You can work within the confines of either situation by focusing your efforts on the members who hold the power at the time.

B. Personal Tools

Summary of Chapters 21–22

- If you live in the United States, you have three members of Congress who represent your interests. Use the power of constituency. Take your problems to your hometown members and build relationships with them. Extend the power of constituency by also building relationships with members who represent others who share your interests. (*Chapter 21*)

- Cultivate a reputation for personal honesty and courtesy in all your dealings with members and staff. Influencing Congress is a long-term activity. A good reputation will serve you well over time. (*Chapter 22*)

Chapter 21

Constituency

I f you reside in any of the fifty United States, then three members of
Congress represent you—two senators and one representative.
They are elected and paid to pursue the interests of their districts.
If you operate an organization in their district, then your interests are
frequently going to coincide with the interests of the district as a whole.

When you have an issue before Congress, always discuss it with
your senators and your representative first before going to other members. First, it is the courteous thing to do. Second, your representatives
have the biggest stake in helping you. If they want to get reelected, they
must look after the interests of their district, particularly its businesses
and other organizations. Third, they will often sit on the committees
that can best help you solve your problem. Surprisingly, many organizations do not talk to their own representatives, and they inevitably fall
behind those who do.

Influencing Congress is a long-term proposition. It is always a good
idea to get to know your local members of Congress and to build ongoing relationships with them. Generally speaking, they will want to
do the same with you. They want to know and keep good employers in
their district. If your organization is considering leaving that district,
your representatives are going to want to know about it.

At times, your representatives may not sit on the right committee
to help you or they may be too junior to have much sway. That does not
mean that they cannot help you. Members build influence within the
Congress by helping other members. Senior members want to help junior members for a variety of reasons. Members can almost always get
the ear of other members, and they will often get a more respectful

hearing than you will. Thus, your representative may be able to talk to an influential member on your behalf when you cannot. Likewise, a member may be able to get the ear of some person in the executive branch when you cannot.

Even if you are not dealing with your own representative, you can still use the power of constituency. For example, you may have a branch office in another member's district. Or you may be a supplier or customer of a major business in a member's district. If so, you should always point out these kinds of connections to a member who is not your representative. It gives them a reason to invest time and political capital in your problem.

Chapter 22

Reputation

As you work to influence Congress, cultivate and preserve your reputation for honesty and fairness. It is the right thing to do, and it also serves your long-term interest. Members of Congress are busy and so are you. Neither you nor they want to waste resources chasing down untruths. Tell the truth, even when it is unfavorable to you. It saves everyone time and money. On the whole, you will get better results if you always deal with members and their staffs honestly.

This works for several reasons. Members see Washington's many shysters and big talkers day in and day out. Those who consistently underpromise and overdeliver provide a pleasant respite from the tide of blather that washes over Congress every day.

A liar has burned every member of Congress at some point, and members have long memories about that sort of thing. Once you lie to them and they find out about it, you will never get on their good side again.

In the same vein, Washington is full of people who are not courteous. Members see those folks every day as well. Courteous dealings with members will make you a welcome visitor. Remember that a member faces dozens of problems and issues at any given time. Your issue will always be the most important one to you, but it may not always be the most important one to the member. Try to see the member's priorities from his or her perspective. Keep to realistic time frames in your requests of members. Do not say your problem is urgent unless it really is. If it is urgent, be prepared to explain precisely why that is and what the consequences of inaction are.

In all your dealings with members and their staffs, look to the future. The long-term damage of a lie or a discourteous act always outweighs the short-term gain.

C. Intellectual Tools

Summary of Chapters 23–27

- Every lobbying effort should have a clear goal from the outset, and all members of the team should be informed of it. Otherwise, lobbyists will simply run up hours, and you will have no way of evaluating whether their actions helped or whether the effort succeeded. (*Chapter 23*)

- The timing of an idea determines its likelihood of success. In any lobbying effort, consider at the outset whether the timing is right for your idea. (*Chapter 24*)

- Think through your positions carefully *before* starting a lobbying effort and ask yourself: is the goal achievable? How long will it take? Do we have the resources to sustain the effort for that period of time? Is our position defensible to those not disposed to like us? Consult a good lobbyist for help in answering these questions and carefully choose the ground you are going to defend. (*Chapter 25*)

- Congress is a Turkish bazaar of policy ideas, many of which make no sense. Put considerable effort into developing good policy solutions; they rise to the top over time. Good ideas embody innovation, simplicity, gains for all stakeholders, incentives, and painlessness. (*Chapter 26*)

- Facts ultimately carry the day in most congressional arguments. Consider your facts carefully before making your arguments. Check the facts relied on by your opponents. Give a human-interest angle to your argument if possible. Keep your arguments simple, sympathetic, and supported by the facts. (*Chapter 27*)

Chapter 23

Goals

ewis Carroll said: "If you do not know where you are going, any road will take you there." One wonders if he was referring to efforts to lobby Congress. In many cases, no one sets a clear goal at the beginning, and therefore no one knows how to direct the effort or whether it succeeded.

These kinds of efforts work well for lobbyists. They can stumble and fumble around going to meetings, reporting back what happened, and collecting a lot of your money without doing you much good. If that happens, it is your fault—not theirs.

In any legislative campaign, first figure out what you want to achieve. Always set a clear goal at the beginning and communicate it clearly to everyone on your team. What the goal is may vary greatly depending on your situation. It may be as broad as getting health-care legislation passed this year or as narrow as getting the effective date changed in the much larger overall bill. You may need to revise your goal as you get into the process and learn what is possible; feel free to do so as circumstances dictate. But when you change your goals, let your team know.

When you have chosen your goal, develop a concrete plan for how you expect to achieve it. For example, are you going to attempt to get your idea through as a freestanding bill? Is it better to try to attach it to some other legislative vehicle that is moving? Will your idea fare better in the Judiciary Committee or the Commerce Committee?

Once you have made these kinds of decisions, make sure you let your entire team know specifically what tasks they are supposed to do and then check to see that they have done them. Do they need to visit a particular member? Do they need to write a letter to all members of a committee? You can change the plan as you go along, but at every step, you should make sure that your team has a definite idea of how the team will try to get to the next step.

In the same vein, always be wary of action for action's sake. You will often find that the next step in your campaign is not obvious or that nothing is happening on your issue. When this happens, lobbyists like to suggest actions. If the suggested action is reasonably likely to change the situation in a positive way, that is well and good. But you should think that question through carefully before taking action. What are the likely consequences of the suggested action? What will it cost? Will it come back to haunt you in six months? Will it spend chits on Capitol Hill that you may need later? If the answers to those questions are not satisfactory, do not fall into the trap of taking an action simply because you cannot think of a way to get your issue moving.

It sounds elementary and it is, but it is often forgotten. If you want to get value for your money in the lobbying world, do not flounder around without direction. Define your goal, make a plan, and see that your team executes it. If it does not work, then figure out why and try again.

Chapter 24

Timing

Victor Hugo said: "There is nothing more powerful than an idea whose time has come." Politics demonstrates this over and over again. Public opinion shifts frequently based on events, sentiments, fashions, and a hundred other things. Ideas that are unpopular one year may become popular next year. Solutions that seem unworkable today may look brilliant two years later.

For example, experts have repeatedly found that the Social Security program cannot remain solvent indefinitely under current law. In 2005, President Bush tried to marshal public support for reforms that he believed would sustain the program far into the future. The effort failed miserably, nothing happened, and Social Security continued on its unsustainable course. The reckoning still looms, however, and it gets closer every day. At some point, a solution will arise, capture significant public support, and pass into law. But the problem is still too far away for most people, and opponents can too easily demagogue the discussion. The time has not yet come.

Contrast that with the regulation of financial services. No one made an issue of sweeping regulatory reform during the flush years before the financial crisis of 2008. Clearly, however, in 2009 and early 2010, the time was ripe because of that crisis.

Your issue may not be as big as Social Security reform or financial services regulation, but it has a timing to it. Pursue your idea when the time is right. The many factors that go into that determination are too complex to give good general advice here. The important point is that you should always consider whether the timing is ripe to push your issue before you spend your money. If it is not, save your issue for a later day.

Chapter 25

Positioning

Before you start your effort to influence Congress, you must carefully think through your position. As Bismarck put it, "politics is the art of the possible." Some things are possible and some are not. Some things are not possible now, but may be in the future. Some complex business bills are possible, but they will take several Congresses to get to a consensus that can be enacted. For example, when the courts broke up AT&T in 1982, Congress spent fourteen years working on legislation to address that situation and finally passed the Telecommunications Act of 1996. As of early 2010, Congress has spent several years working on patent reform—thus far with no new law.

If what you want is never going to be possible, then you are wasting your money trying to get it. If what you want is going to take several Congresses, then you have to consider whether it is worth that level of effort and money.

To any leader of an organization who is not immersed in the workings of Congress, distinguishing between those categories may be difficult. Good lobbyists can walk you through this decision. They should talk to you about what is realistic up front. If they do not, consider another one. Granted, this is not an exact science, but your lobbyist should at least discuss it with you.

If you believe that your goal is possible, then by all means, go forward. But think about how your rhetoric and substantive position will sound to people who may not know you or like you. Think about how your congressional supporters will look if they adopt your position. Think about how the public will perceive what you have to say. Can you explain yourself in terms that the average adult can understand? The same fundamentally defensible substantive position may win or lose depending on the rhetoric you use.

If you believe that your goal is not possible, then do not waste your time and money. Organizations frequently pursue goals that are clearly not within reach from the perspective of anyone who knows what is going on. For example, medical malpractice reform measures are unlikely to pass in a Democratic Congress. A health-care system administered by the federal government is unlikely to pass in a Republican Congress. If that is the situation, take another look at your situation. See if some smaller, more attainable action will help. Congress and individual members have many ways to achieve their goals—not all of them require passing a law.

If your goal is not possible now, but might be in the future, then it is a question of how much time and money you have to spend. Only you can make that decision in the context of a particular situation. However, a good lobbyist can give you some advice on what the parameters of your situation are.

Most importantly, do not defeat yourself at the start by locking yourself into a losing position. Worse yet, do not damage your situation further by adopting an indefensible position. Choose carefully the ground you are going to defend—it is one of the few things in this process that you can control.

Chapter 26

Quality
of Ideas

Supreme Court Justice Oliver Wendell Holmes once said: "The best test of truth is the power of the thought to get itself accepted in the competition of the market." Congress is a Turkish bazaar of policy ideas. Many of them make no sense. In the short term, many of these bad ideas get enacted for any number of reasons. Often it is the almost irresistible urge to do something—no matter how ill-conceived—in the face of a crisis.

In the long run, however, good ideas rise to the top. Put some serious thought into the policy solution you will propose. You are paid to pursue the interests of your organization and you should do so. But getting anything done in Congress requires bringing many people together.

You can produce better policy ideas in several ways. Policies that serve only the naked self-interest of your business or your industry fool no one. As Adam Smith put it: "People of the same trade seldom meet together, even for merriment and diversion, but the conversation ends in a conspiracy against the public, or in some contrivance to raise prices."

While the policy ideas before Congress are many and varied, they often plow the same old intellectual furrows. If you can come up with something truly new, it will be welcomed.

Simple ideas usually work best. Warren Buffett says you should not invest in a business if you do not understand what it does. Transfer that thought to a member of Congress. If you were a member, would you want to invest your political capital in a policy idea that you cannot understand or explain? Remember that the politicians will have to go out and explain it to a skeptical public.

Your ideas are more likely to succeed when they create win-win situations for all the interested stakeholders. Look at your situation and see if you can create that dynamic. Likewise, if you are opposing a particular idea, show members why it creates losers.

Think about how you can give people legal incentives to act rather than simply throwing money at a problem. As our national debt reaches truly epic dimensions, solutions that require more government money are going to be ever harder to sell. We simply do not have the money. The wave of the future will be incentives associated with low cost.

If you want people to comply with some regulatory regime, think about how you can make it easy for them to do so. Politicians hate to inflict pain on their constituents. If you can eliminate any pain for constituents, you will have more luck selling your idea.

For congressional purposes, quality ideas embody innovation, simplicity, gains for all stakeholders, incentives, and little pain for constituents. Few situations have solutions that encompass all of these traits, but you should aim for as many of them as you can achieve.

Chapter 27

Facts and Arguments

Facts persuade. You can use a lot of high-flown rhetoric, but over the long run, the facts usually carry the day. One killer fact can propel your bill all the way to the president's desk. For example, in early 2009, broadcast television stations were approaching a deadline for switching to digital broadcasting. Many Americans were unprepared for the switch and would have had no television afterwards. That fact quickly led to passage of a four-month extension. The DTV Delay Act, Pub. L. No. 111-4, 123 Stat. 112 (2009).

By the same token, a killer fact on the other side can sink your efforts before you get started. For example, during the effort to pass healthcare reform legislation in the summer and fall of 2009, various proposals died when the Congressional Budget Office estimated their cost as higher than expected.

As you choose your position—before you start your efforts—carefully study the facts of the situation. Pick up them up, shake them around, and look at them from all angles. Congress will do this once you start pushing your idea, and you will be better off if you have thought through all the angles.

Most people believe that everyone else will see the facts the same way they do. Members and their staffs come from all sorts of backgrounds that differ from yours. They care about all sorts of things that you do not care about. Many of them will see your situation differently than you do. They may question your motives or your honesty. Always respond calmly and return to the facts if this happens.

When trying to assemble your case persuasively, first ensure that your assertions of fact are truthful. If you get caught lying or even shading the truth, your credibility will be shot. Members and staff will question everything else you say.

For the same reason, check your opponents' assertions of facts carefully. Many people forget to do this. They let the other side give out false information and thereby hurt their own cause. If you catch your opponents in an error, you do not need to call them names. Simply point out the inaccuracy and provide whatever backup you can.

Members like real people and human-interest stories. If you can give your story a compelling human-interest angle, you are more likely to succeed. Members respond more favorably to a real human need than to a stack of statistical data. For this reason, bills that remedy some deficiency in the criminal justice system frequently bear the name of a crime victim who suffered because of the deficiency, as in Jessica's Law. And remember the congressional frenzies surrounding the Elian Gonzalez and Terri Schiavo cases described in Chapter 11.

As you approach a member or a staffer, you should emphasize those parts of your story that appeal to that individual. Democrats may like one part of your story, and Republicans may like another. Feel free to shift emphasis as you move from one person to another. If you are presenting your story to someone and they show particular interest in one aspect of it, then focus on that aspect. The goal is not to get through the script of your presentation, but to persuade that person. If they indicate that they are not persuaded by one part of your story, then by all means move to another part.

Members and their staffs face many issues every day. They only have a limited amount of time to spend on any given issue. For that reason, simplicity is the coin of the realm on Capitol Hill. If you can state your position in twenty-five words or less, you are much better off. Easily remembered bumper-sticker slogans generally work better than 1,000-page treatises dense with data.

In making your arguments, you should always remember that members and their staffers listen to pitches about federal policy all day long. They hear hundreds of them. Rhetoric generally will not impress them, and it simply wastes the small amount of time you will have to spend on them.

The same is true for talk of personalities. If a member or a staffer has served for long, they have seen all types—from the wonderful to the sleazy to the downright bizarre. They quickly come to recognize them and accept them as a fact of life. They may know your opponents much better than you do. Speaking ill of them runs the risk that the member or staffer may think differently of that person and then wonder about you.

In making your affirmative case, remember that most congressional issues involve both a problem and a solution. If you are the proponent of an idea, you must persuade members and their staffs that a problem in fact exists and that your solution to it is the right one. So you must give thought to both aspects. Be prepared to answer questions about why your proposed solution solves the problem and what its effect is on other people—particularly whatever people the member or staffer cares about. If you are the opponent, your job is easier. Then you can win by convincing them that no problem exists or that the proposed solution is not the right one. You only have to win on one.

Several arguments apply to almost all issues. One is cost. We have huge budget deficits and no money for new spending, particularly after the various efforts to address the financial crisis of 2008. If you are the proponent of an idea, you are better off if it does not cost the government anything. Failing that, you are better off if its cost can be paid out of some existing pot of money. If you oppose the idea, you almost always have some kind of cost argument. Cost need not necessarily be a direct cost to the government. You can also argue that the idea imposes costs on state and local governments or private actors.

If your idea involves some dedicated funding source like a user fee, then it becomes a question of who will bear the cost. If you are the proponent, then your best argument will be that whoever truly benefits will bear the cost. If you are the opponent, your best argument will be that the idea places the cost on someone who should not have to bear it—preferably someone the member or staffer cares about.

Another argument is the level of controversy. In general, members do not like to choose between various factions. As they like to say on Capitol Hill, "I have friends on both sides and I like to be on the side with my friends." If you are the proponent of an idea, you want to be able to argue that your solution satisfies everyone and a vote will not cause controversy. If you oppose the idea, you want to say that you and others are not satisfied and will be mad if the member votes for it.

Another argument that applies widely is that the solution's time has or has not come. Congress can only deal with so many issues during any given two-year session. Thus, if you are the proponent of an idea, you must always argue that the time for it has arrived and the process should move forward without delay. If you are the opponent of an idea, delay is your friend. The reasons for delay are infinite. They include: no hearing has been held on the bill; the bill has not been sufficiently vetted with the interested parties; the bill needs tweaking; and the bill should wait on some external development like a court decision. The list goes on, but you get the idea.

Another argument that comes up quite often is that the proposal rewards bad behavior. Proponents must show that whatever group gets a benefit deserves it, based on the group's past behavior. Opponents must argue that whatever group is getting the benefit did something wrong, that it does not deserve the benefit, and that giving it the benefit will only encourage more bad behavior.

Many business issues involve the level-playing-field argument. The proponent will argue that it does not want any special treatment. Rather, it wants to take away some special advantage that its competitor has and achieve a level playing field so that all may compete fairly. The opponent will usually argue that either the field is already level or the situation involves two completely different fields. Obviously, this one is in the eye of the beholder.

Another argument is precedent. Members and staff frequently like to follow some prior example rather than blazing a new trail. This rarely involves a deep analysis of the success of the prior example, but the comfort is real. If you are the proponent of an idea, it often helps to say that this is just like something that you did five years ago. If you are the opponent, you want to say that the proposal is completely unprecedented.

A variation of the precedent argument is that a proposal will open the floodgates for similar laws in other situations. Here the argument is not so much about past precedent, but rather what precedent this proposal sets for the future. If you are the proponent of the idea, you will want to argue that the proposal pertains only to this situation. If you are the opponent, you want to argue that many similar groups will come back next year expecting something similar and no reasonable distinction exists.

A variation of the precedent argument occurs when some existing program is being amended or reauthorized. If you are the proponent of the program, you argue that it has worked well and it just needs a few tweaks. If you are the opponent, you argue that it has not worked well and should be ended.

Finally, you can argue the specter of unintended consequences for almost any proposal. Because so many laws cause them, the opponent of a proposal can easily, and often effectively, gin up some parade of potential horribles. Because this exercise necessarily rests on speculation, a proponent may find it hard to counter. But this can sometimes work to the advantage of a proponent when the proposal fixes the unintended consequence of an earlier law.

These examples give you a sense of the vast territory over which most congressional arguments occur. A variety of other arguments that typically appeal to one party or the other are too numerous to list here, but if you follow politics at all, you will quickly get a sense of them.

Whatever your argument is, you must present it to members and staff to have any impact. When you meet with them, it is a good practice to have a simple, one-page summary of your argument in writing. If the essence of your argument cannot fit on one page, you are probably wasting your time. If possible, send it to the member or staffer ahead of time. Whether you have sent it ahead of time or not, bring it to the meeting with you and give it to them at the beginning of the meeting so they can follow along. Be sure to put it on your web site in a policy section so that they can read it later when they have the time but cannot find the paper you gave them.

As you are making your pitch, listen to the questions. They will tell you what the person cares about. They may also reveal the weaknesses in your argument. They will often let you know what your opponents are saying. That can be valuable information. If you cannot answer a question, admit it, promise to get back to the person, and do get back to the person with the answer. If you cannot answer a question because your case is weak on a particular point, get with others on your side and try to develop a better answer. If you cannot do that, think about tweaking your proposal in some way that makes the question go away.

Members and their staffs hear hundreds of pitches. Those that stand out and win the day are simple, sympathetic, and supported by the facts.

D. Environmental Tools

Summary of Chapters 28–30

- The legislative market of Congress responds to political signals just like economic markets respond to price signals. Hire a good lobbyist to help you read those signals. You will not have the time to learn how to decipher them. (*Chapter 28*)

- The more allies you have on your side, the more likely you are to get your way. Recruit allies by thinking about who shares your interests and do not forget to go beyond the obvious. Expect everyone who joins a cause to participate, and do not let allies free-ride on your efforts. Do not have meetings unless there are specific matters to address. (*Chapter 29*)

- To get anything done in Congress, you need members to act as your champions. Choosing the right champion depends on the circumstances of the situation, but once you have chosen a member as a champion, stick close to that member. (*Chapter 30*)

Chapter 28

Signals

J ust as economic markets respond to price signals, the legislative market on Capitol Hill responds to political signals. To influence Congress, you must heed those signals. Listening to them and acting accordingly can substantially advance your cause.

Actors in the process often send these signals in the form of deliberate public statements. But they may be sent more subtly through taking actions or not taking them. A vote, a story leaked to the press, a question at a hearing, a key player's presence at a press conference, and a chairman's timing for scheduling a hearing can all signal what is going on behind the scenes and what the outcome of a legislative struggle will be. Some signals are sent in code; some are worded broadly when something specific is meant; and some can be quite direct.

You likely do not have time to listen to or decipher all the signals pertaining to your issue. Indeed, you likely do not even have time to pull the signals about your issue from the much broader mass of signals that flow from Congress every day. You would not be using your time efficiently if you did.

This is one place where a good lobbyist can add a lot of value to your efforts. Deciphering congressional signals is like understanding Morse Code or signaling with flags; you do not have to be a genius to do it, but it does require some initial know-how and then continued practice. If you stop practicing, you lose the ability just like you lose a foreign language.

In addition, the meaning of political signals depends on the larger context in which they are sent. What a signal means today depends on

what happened yesterday and what is expected to happen next week. To read them accurately, you must follow the story line every day.

Many false signals—usually in the form of unfounded rumor—also get sent every day in Congress. You will save yourself a lot of time, money, and headache if you avoid responding to false signals. When you hear a rumor, ask yourself whether the underlying substance of the rumor makes any sense. If it does not, then the rumor is probably not true. If the rumor begins with the idea that a particular person said or did something, try to verify the rumor with that person before you act on it. You will be surprised how many times you will reach the person and they will not have said or done anything remotely like what you have heard.

When many people are awaiting a decision on something, it is common to hear many conflicting rumors about what the decision will be. Usually, that means that the decision has not yet been made. When the rumors start to converge to the same substance, that usually means the decision has been made.

Non-lobbyists do not have time to wade through all these signals, but it is the stock in trade of lobbyists. Hiring a lobbyist to read the signals is some of the best money you will spend in this process. Spend it and your cause will reap the benefits.

Chapter 29

Allies

As former Rep. Henry Hyde used to say, "We win here by addition—not subtraction." He was referring to votes, of course, but the same is true of any effort to influence Congress. Congress responds to pressure—the more groups and people that you have on your side, the more likely you are to get your way.

When you start with a new issue, give some thought to who shares your interest on the issue. Ask those in your company who are directly affected by the issue who your allies might be. It is not always obvious. They may be able to take you beyond the first level and point out less obvious targets.

Having identified your allies, get in touch with those people and try to enlist them in the cause. Surprisingly, many times they will not even be aware of the issue. Like you, they have many things to keep up with. Even lobbyists, who study every move Congress makes, cannot keep up with everything. Congress is just too big, and it is involved in too many issues. Do not assume that your allies know about and are already working on the problem. Get the word out and assume that those who have conflicting interests are busily doing the same.

Find out whether your targets care about the issue and whether they will put any resources into it. Many times, they will say they have an interest, but it is just not important enough to spend any money on or they do not have the resources to take it on. Companies are often more than willing to free-ride on your efforts, particularly if the issue is not particularly urgent or it looks like nothing will happen in the near future. You may avoid that problem if you approach someone in the company whom the issue directly affects. That may get more action

than going to a company lobbyist who does not want one more issue added to an already overstuffed portfolio.

Think about trade associations in addition to individual companies. Check with any trade associations that you belong to and see what they are doing. That may provide an opportunity for you to get some more value for what you are paying them. Also, check with the trade associations of any companies who have said that they are interested, but cannot get involved for one reason or another.

Once you have a list of who is actually willing to do something, get those people together in a room and develop a plan. Make sure that everyone in the group carries part of the financial burden and no one takes a free ride. Assign tasks and put someone in charge of seeing that they are done.

Many such groups have regular meetings to go over these sorts of things. You only need to hold these kinds of meetings when you have a specific task to accomplish. Washington lobbyists like to go to these kinds of meetings because they can rely on their attendance to justify their existence. In most of them, not much happens. Assigning tasks and having the chair follow up by email or phone is a more effective way of getting things done.

Despite their shortcomings, participating in coalitions with those who share your interests will help you influence Congress.[13]

---

13. See Chapters 31–34, for some of the practical tools that coalitions can use to communicate their message.

Chapter 30

The Champion

You cannot take part in the actual workings of Congress. Only members of Congress can speak on the floor, vote, and otherwise participate in its official activities. To get anything done in those official activities, you have to get a member to act for you. While various members may play some role in your issue, it is always best if you have a champion.

A champion invests political capital in your issue and will see it through the vicissitudes of the legislative process. Champions take on issues for various reasons. The issue may be important to their district. It may relate to their previous profession or to a concern of a family member or a close friend. It may be important to a group they are courting. Or it may simply interest them intellectually.

You can have more than one champion. In a perfect world, you would like to have at least one from each party in each chamber. That is not always possible, but it is a good goal to strive for.

Sometimes when you start with a new issue, the choice of your champion will be obvious because of the history of the industry or the related issues. Or you may come into an issue after the legislative process has started and you may already have an existing champion. If either is the case, then it is usually best to go with that existing champion to avoid giving offense and to maximize the benefits of the champion's past experience.

At other times, the choice will not be so clear. If that is the case, the choice is important to your strategy and you should consider it carefully. Generally speaking, if your issue is a large and complex one that Congress is sure to address, then you will want to enlist the chairs of the relevant committees if possible. If you know they are opposed to you, then your next best champion may be the ranking member of the relevant committee. On rare occasions, a party leader may champion an issue, but this usually happens only when the issue matters to the leader's district or will likely affect an upcoming election.

If your issue can be dealt with by an amendment to a major bill, then you may choose one of the senior members of the relevant committee. When a major bill is going through Congress, the chair and ranking member cannot take on every sub-issue within the bill. They need help from some of the other members and that may be your opportunity.

If your issue is smaller and less controversial, you may want to look to a more junior member of a relevant committee. Senior members like to farm out smaller issues to younger members to give them a chance to develop their legislative skills. When junior members face a tough reelection battle, more senior members may give an issue to them to help their reelection campaigns.

If all of the above fails, get whatever member you can. Even if the member is not on a relevant committee and is not a senior member, it is still better to have a champion than not to have one.

Having chosen a champion and gotten that member committed to your issue, you should work closely and consult with your champion on all major strategic steps. Your champion will be looking to you for guidance and help, but the member can also provide you with valuable intelligence. They can also talk to other members on your behalf when you are unable to reach them.

In short, get some champions, stick close to them, and give them all the credit for whatever gets accomplished.

E. Practical Tools

Summary of Chapters 31–34

- Congress generally is not corrupt. You can give campaign money legally in a way that advances your goals. Do not look at campaign contributions as a means of achieving a particular end, but as a means of building a long-term relationship with a member. (*Chapter 31*)

- Grassroots efforts have the power to move Congress, but they are difficult to activate on most issues. (*Chapter 32*)

- Grasstops (VIP) pressure can also persuade Congress. Think broadly about who may be a VIP in a particular situation. Once VIPs are identified and motivated to act, use them to get your message across to the members you need to persuade. (*Chapter 33*)

- The Internet can be an excellent tool for reaching Congress, but it is only a conduit for your message. It cannot improve an unpersuasive message. (*Chapter 34*)

Chapter 31

Money

Many believe that Congress does business based on suitcases full of cash that corporations pass to members. Such things happen from time to time, and those involved appropriately go to jail. But they are the exception, not the rule. Most lobbyists and members conduct their business legally.

You should always approach Congress honestly, and if anybody suggests otherwise, run from the room as fast as you can. Congress cannot give you or your organization anything that is worth your going to prison.

Having said that, it still costs money to run for office—tons of money. Indeed, it was the brazen pursuit of tons of money during the 1972 Nixon presidential reelection campaign that led to the famous Watergate phrase: "Follow the money." In those days of lax oversight, suitcases full of cash did change hands. But in today's world, extensive regulation and a huge increase in the number of people who are watching have, for the most part, ended that sort of thing.

Nonetheless, contributing to campaigns within the bounds of the law can help your relationship with a member. You should never look at contributions as in anticipation of, or in return for, any specific action a member may take. Nor should you look at them as all you need to get what you want. Rather, you should look at campaign contributions as one of a number of ways of building a long-term relationship with a member.

Having decided to give legitimate contributions to a member, you still must figure out how to do it. There are many opportunities to donate. Fund-raising events typically involve a meal with the member that lasts about an hour to an hour and a half. These events provide good opportunities to get to know the member. Most members have a fund-raising event every month or two if not more frequently. If you suddenly discover that you need to get to know a member, showing up at the member's next fund-raiser allows you to get to know him or her in the short term.

During the event, the member will often let the donors briefly say what is on their minds. This is a good time to apprise the member of your issue, but not to discuss it at length unless the member encourages it. Sometimes, everyone at a fund-raiser will care about the same set of issues. Then it is more appropriate to talk about that issue in more detail. Generally, though, you should keep it brief and not monopolize the conversation. You are looking for the member either to say something positive about your issue or to have someone on the staff follow up with you. If the member points you in that direction, follow up with the staffer, but do not mention that you gave to the campaign.

In fact, you should never mention any campaign contribution when dealing with a staffer on a substantive issue. Generally, only one or two of the member's top staffers participate in the political fund-raising. They receive constant pressure to raise money for a variety of political causes. You can rest assured that they are very much aware of who has helped. You never need to bring it up with them or anyone else on the member's official government staff. If you have a problem related to fund-raising, raise it with the member's fund-raiser or campaign staff.

There are various other types of fund-raisers. Some members will have fund-raisers that are receptions, as they are known in Washington. Most of the rest of the world knows them as cocktail parties. Often, events in the member's district will be of this type. These tend to be larger events where you will have less time to speak to the member. If you want to talk to a member about an issue, these are not the best events to do it. But if you are going just to show support, these events suffice for that purpose.

More senior members sometimes sponsor weekend trips for big

donors. These may be to the member's district, to some vacation spot, or to some big sports or musical event. These events cost you more because the required contribution will be higher and you will have to pay your own travel expenses. However, they allow you to spend some relaxed time with a member and get to know them much better than you could at a regular fund-raiser. You may also have the chance to speak to the member about your issue at more length.

You may also get calls from members when they are raising money for political causes other than their own. In particular, most senior members have to raise money for their party's campaign committee every year to maintain their leadership positions. Contributors often complain that they do not like to give to the party because they do not get any credit for it. On the contrary, however, members often struggle to raise this money. They especially appreciate donors who help them raise this money. Moreover, these kinds of donations usually allow you to go to large events where you will have the opportunity to speak to many members. From a credit perspective, they are a bonus, not a burden.

Senior members may also hold fund-raisers for other members who are in close races. The same logic applies to these fund-raisers. It is often hard money to raise, from the senior member's perspective. If you give, you get credit from both members and you get to talk to both at the event.

If you get into the fund-raising game, you will get many more requests than you could ever possibly meet. Thus, you need to make some sort of strategic plan about how to spend whatever money you have to give. You should always give to your local members. Beyond that, you want to give the bulk of your money to the members who are in the best position to help you. Often that will be obvious based on what industry you are in or what the issue of the moment is. If it is not, a good lobbyist should be able to help you with that.

If a member calls you asking for money and you take the call, be polite and be honest. If, for whatever reason you cannot give this time, say you cannot, but say keep me in mind for next time or something along that line. Members get told no a lot and they expect it. Do not

promise money that you are not going to deliver. If you need to check with someone and get back to the member, say so. Then get back to the member's fund-raiser even if the answer is negative. Nothing is more frustrating for the member than to think the goal is made only to have someone not come through at the last moment. You should underpromise and overdeliver.

Apart from contributions, there are also gifts. Until fairly recently, ethics rules were fairly lax about giving gifts or meals to members and staff. As a result of the Honest Leadership and Open Government Act (known as "HLOGA") and other changes, the rules are now much tighter. If you are not an expert in the details of the rules, the best rule of thumb is not to pay for anything for a member or a staffer.

The complexities of what you can and cannot legally do in this arena are far beyond the scope of this book. Suffice it to say that the law in this area often runs counter to what common sense would tell you. Just because it seems like it must be legal does not mean that it is. If you are going to participate in any significant way, you should definitely invest your money in retaining competent counsel to advise you.[14]

---

14. For more information on the legalities of campaign contributions and gifts, see § 2.3 of *Lobbying and Advocacy* entitled "Recommended Resources: Determining Compliance with Key Lobbying and Ethics Requirements."

Chapter 32

Grassroots

I n the congressional context, the term "grassroots" refers to some group of average people who care enough about an issue to contact their member. The group may be as large as all senior citizens or it may be as small as the employees of one company.

Grassroots efforts can move Congress profoundly. Congress is designed to respond to pressure and it does. One recent example was the debate over immigration reform in the summer of 2007. So many people called the Senate to oppose the bill that the switchboard crashed. Needless to say, the bill did not pass.

As that episode illustrates, grassroots pressure effectively influences Congress when it is activated. The trick, however, is to get it activated. For most people, Congress is of little concern in their daily lives. If they think of it at all, they probably feel disdain or contempt. To get average people to contact members, your issue must directly affect their lives or concern some visceral feeling they have. For example, try something that negatively affects people's televisions or their guns and you will get an understanding of what "visceral" really means. Unfortunately, most issues do not fall into these categories except when jobs are at stake.

For that reason, grassroots efforts have limited utility for most issues. But let's assume you have an issue that can attract grassroots support. To start, you must identify the affected group of people. Then you must communicate with them about the issue and why it affects them. This short communication must be phrased in language that average people can understand. Then you must tell them what to say to their member and how to do it. Make it as easy as possible.

Generally speaking, communications in the person's own language have more impact on members than canned words. However, if you are trying to get a large number of people to contact members, most are not going to take the time to fashion their own message. A canned message is better than no message at all. And a large number of canned messages do have an effect. Remember that members avidly read their hometown newspapers, and your grassroots efforts can speak to them there as well. A well-placed letter to the editor or opinion piece can catch their eye.

When most people speak of grassroots pressure, they are thinking about persuading a large part of Congress to behave in a certain way. However, you can also use grassroots pressure for more limited purposes. At times, you may only need to move one particular member or a few. In those cases, it may be easier to activate the grassroots.

Some companies are in the business of helping interest groups stir up grassroots pressure on Congress. These are perfectly legitimate businesses and it is fine to use them if you have the money to do so. Just be sure that you are dealing with a reputable company. Phony grassroots efforts, also known as Astroturf, can severely damage your cause if you get caught. No one likes to be played for a fool.[15]

---

15. For more detail on grassroots, see Chapter 7 of *Lobbying and Advocacy* entitled "Develop, Never Devalue, Grassroots."

Chapter 33

Grasstops

You may not be as familiar with the term "grasstops." In the lobbying world, it refers to efforts to influence Congress through contacts with corporate CEOs and other VIPs. In this context, though, VIP is a loose term. For example, if the American Medical Association seeks to persuade Congress of something, the VIPs may be the members' personal doctors. Or a member may have a friend whom the member believes knows more than anyone on the subject. The member may listen to that person and no one else on a particular issue.

Like grassroots efforts, grasstops efforts can persuade members and staff. Like most of us, members and staffers like to meet and talk to VIPs. It is part of the fun of the job.

But grasstops pressure can also be hard to activate. CEOs are busy people and they do not have time to call members unless the issue matters a lot to the company. If the situation involves personal doctors or friends or something of that sort, it may be difficult to identify who those people are.

In most cases, however, organizations have an easier time applying grasstops pressure than grassroots pressure because organizations control their own leaders. Those leaders will usually know who within their sphere shares their interests and what other prominent leaders may be interested.

Basically, you face three issues when you are trying to activate grasstops pressure. Which members are you trying to influence? Whom do they listen to? And within that group of people that those members listen to, who has sufficient interest to make the contact? Once you have thought through those questions, the way forward will usually be fairly clear.

If you have decided which VIP should contact which member, then you need to work out the time and place. A personal meeting works best if the timing of the issue allows it and the VIP can get to the member. You can do this in the member's office if that is convenient, but it need not necessarily happen there. It can take place at a social event, a charity dinner, or wherever the two may happen to meet. If time is short or the VIP is across the country, a phone call is the next best option. Most members will make time for a short conversation with a VIP within a day or two.

However the contact occurs, the principles discussed in Chapter 35 on meetings apply even more forcefully in this situation. Hone the VIP's message to the bare essentials and get right to the point. Members are busy people and you will waste the opportunity if the VIP spends too much time dawdling over pleasantries.

VIPs can have a significant impact on members. Organizations should use them when and where appropriate.

Chapter 34

The Internet

The Internet provides us with an ability to communicate that we could not even dream of a few years ago. You can certainly use that resource in efforts to influence Congress.

You can email members of Congress as well as individuals who share your interests. You can put up websites that educate the public, members, and staff about your issue. You can post videos and comment on news stories. You can even have your own blogs and social networking tools to spread your thoughts.

Use the Internet to the maximum when you try to influence Congress. However, you should keep a few things in mind. The Internet is an incredibly powerful and flexible tool, but it is only a conduit for getting your message out to the world. No matter how far and wide the Internet distributes your message, it does not improve the quality or persuasiveness of your message. And the Internet is forever. Once you put a flawed product out there, it can be hard to get it back. Think through your message carefully before you broadcast it to the world.

By the same token, posting something on the Internet does not mean anybody gets your message. Lots of people blog or tweet about what they had for lunch today and nobody else reads what they have said. Put your message on the Internet in a way that reaches those people you are trying to influence. If you are trying to reach members of Congress, email them instead of placing an ad in some publication that you assume they must all read. If you are going to blog about something, then do something to make your targets aware of your blog.

Finally, as with grassroots efforts, do not put phony stuff on the Internet or send made-up emails. Think about how embarrassed you

will be when a member goes to the floor to read a message generated by your company and then reveals that the member knew the sender of the message personally and that person died five years ago. Those sorts of things happen from time to time and you do not want your company involved.

F. Opportunities

Summary of Chapters 35–40

- Seek a meeting with a member only when you have something important to say or you need the member to decide a major strategic question. Think through what you hope to accomplish in the meeting. Hone your message to the bare essentials and get right to the point. Meetings with members are often interrupted by other events. If at all possible, agree with staff as you leave the meeting on how best to follow up. (*Chapter 35*)

- Hearings are the way that congressional committees formally educate themselves about issues. Unless there is a compelling reason not to do it, testify at hearings when asked to do so. (*Chapter 36*)

- Markups are the time when a congressional committee meets to discuss, amend, and vote on legislation. Constant communication and sharing of information are the keys to working successfully with committee allies to achieve the desired result in the markup. (*Chapter 37*)

- Floor consideration is not automatic just because a bill passes out of a committee. Think from the beginning about how you will convince party leaders to give your bill floor time. If you oppose a bill, try to create as much delay and controversy as you can to convince leaders not to bring it up. (*Chapter 38*)

- Conference committees often insert language into bills that could not otherwise be passed. Thus, conferences are times of great danger and opportunity. Generally, party leaders and committee chairs will control what goes into the conference committee's final product. You must build relationships with those members to protect yourself during a conference. (*Chapter 39*)

- When faced with a crisis, Congress wants to legislate and legislate fast. A crisis situation is similar to a conference. You must build relationships with party leaders and committee chairs to protect yourself from unfavorable items that may be inserted into must-pass "crisis" legislation. (*Chapter 40*)

Chapter 35

The Meeting

Meetings with members of Congress can often advance your cause if conducted properly. But these limited opportunities are often wasted. Many meetings with members end with the member and the staffer having no idea why the visitor was there. If you are going to meet with a member of Congress, have something important to say.

If you are a legitimate leader of an organization with a serious issue, most members of Congress are going to make time to see you. Thus, do not fall victim to the lobbyist who has nothing to offer you beyond getting you in to see a member. But understand from the outset that on most issues, you are only going to get one or two chances to meet with the member directly.

Most members have a staff person whose primary responsibility is to keep up with the member's schedule. Contact that person to arrange the meeting. These staffers lead chaotic lives, so do not be insulted if they do not respond immediately. Members have a variety of procedures relating to how they schedule the meetings. For example, some care very much about exactly who will be in the meeting; others do not.

If the scheduler asks you to fill out a form, do it accurately and return it on a timely basis. If there is a valid reason why the meeting needs to happen immediately, let the scheduler know the time frame, but otherwise do not demand a meeting urgently. Make friends with the scheduler and understand the constant juggling that person must do. The more lead time you can give the scheduler, the better. You should also let the staffer responsible for the substance of your issue know you are going to schedule a meeting with the member and provide them with any relevant information about the issue.

Suppose that you have decided that now is the time to meet with a member. Before you call the scheduler, ask yourself what you hope to accomplish in the meeting and whether it is realistic. Think about what position your message puts the member in and how the member is likely to respond. Think about whether you should have this meeting with the member or with the relevant staff member. Generally, you want to schedule meetings with members to get them to make major strategic decisions. You want to schedule meetings with staff when you want to get into details.

In thinking about the meeting, keep in mind that members have dozens of commitments and issues to attend to every day. Generally they are only going to meet with you for a brief time—usually five to fifteen minutes, at most thirty. Many times, you may have that much time on the member's schedule, but three minutes into the meeting, the bells signifying a floor vote will ring or the scheduler will notify the member that some VIP is calling and the member must take the call. The member then cuts your meeting short.

For all these reasons, you must hone your message to its bare essentials. Most members expect to exchange pleasantries at the beginning of a meeting. You should do this, but keep it to the absolute minimum. It wastes your valuable time with the member. Too many times, executives who have not lobbied much start telling stories and never get to the point of the meeting.

If you have employees who live or work in the member's district, know how many and tell the member that at the beginning of the meeting. You do not have to dwell on it unless the issue pertains directly to those employees, but that statement will always get a member's attention.

Pick the two or three main points of your argument and explain them to the member in language that an average newspaper reader can understand. Members are perfectly capable of understanding most issues in more detail, but they are not going to have the time to master them. Many people try to explain every detail of their world to the member before getting to the issue at hand and they waste the whole meeting.

If the member asks you a question, answer it as directly as you can. You will only annoy the member if you waste time dancing around a question. If the member's question reveals a weakness in your argument, admit it candidly and move back to your strengths as quickly as possible. If you do not know the answer, say that you do not, but that you will get the requested information to the member. If you say you will follow up with information, send it. Many people fail to do that and it makes the member feel you were simply "checking the box."

Do not criticize whatever group opposes you. You may believe that they are bad people, but again this wastes your valuable time with the member and accomplishes nothing. Counter their arguments as best you can and move on.

Then move to your ask—whatever it may be. Most times, you are not going to get a direct answer in the meeting. The member will want to think about your request. Ask when and how you can follow up rather than demanding an answer at the time of the meeting. Often, you will have a chance to talk to the staffer alone as you leave the member's office. That is usually a good time to reach a clear understanding on how to follow up or when you should check back.[16]

---

16. For more information on meetings, see §§ 8.26–8.36 of *Lobbying and Advocacy*.

Chapter 36

The Hearing

Congress's substantive work occurs in committees. As they do that work, members and staff educate themselves in many ways. The most formal way is to hold a committee hearing. The mechanics of how a hearing works are set forth in Appendix D.

Beyond the basic parameters explained there, hearings are fairly free-wheeling affairs, and the discussion tends to range broadly over the topics within the general issue area. The hearing notice will indicate whether the hearing will focus on a specific piece of legislation or a topic area on which the committee is considering drafting legislation. In the latter case, it may be called an oversight hearing although for all practical purposes it may be legislative in nature.

Committees also hold hearings that are more accurately described as oversight hearings. They may look at a particular agency's overall performance or some specific problem that has come to light. These kinds of hearings can be a good time to bring an issue to the attention of an agency head who may be testifying if you can get a friendly member to ask a question for you. At any rate, the formalities are not that important so long as you understand what the committee is trying to get at. What is important is to make your affirmative case as persuasively as you can.

Organizations often shy away from testifying at hearings because they fear that members will ask them tough questions or that the press will write unfavorable stories. Avoiding testifying at a congressional hearing is generally a mistake. For one thing, press attention varies widely depending on the perceived news value of the topic and the witnesses. What may seem like a momentous issue to you may put the press to sleep and vice versa. Some hearings will have a dozen television cameras rolling. Others will only have a handful of tourists in the audience. Keep in mind, though, that most hearings are webcast over the Internet nowadays, and so there may be a much larger audience watching live that is not in the room. It is hard to predict in advance how much interest a hearing will draw, but it is easy to predict that the committee members and staff will not appreciate your refusal to testify.

Apart from that, a well-prepared and articulate witness can help advance your cause in a hearing. The military axiom that "prior preparation prevents poor performance" definitely applies here. Members often ask unfair questions or otherwise showboat during hearings. But you get the chance to explain your case to members, the press, and the world. The setting ensures that you will get more attention than in almost any other place. In most circumstances, you do better by getting into the arena and giving as good as you get than by hiding from any public dialogue at all.

For example, with businesses, most people forget that whatever sins businesses may commit, they still provide us with most of our daily needs. Providing products we need is often difficult and expensive. You can make that argument forcefully in a congressional hearing. The same is true for the rest of your case.

A hearing may also reveal where you stand with members. You will often learn what members whose positions are unknown are thinking. You then have the opportunity to speak to their concerns and persuade them of your point of view. A hearing can also show you and your opponents the strengths and weaknesses of your respective cases. Press coverage of the hearing can tell you more about how the press and public feel about your issue. It may also recruit new allies to your cause. In short, organizations generally shrink from making their affirmative case in a hearing and lose its many benefits.

In some cases, you may face a different problem. You may desperately want to testify, but the committee may not have enough slots to let you. In that case, you can first make your case as to what you can add to the hearing, but put it in terms of what will make a better hearing for the committee rather than how it will help you. If that fails, ask if you can submit a written statement for the record. Most committees allow that without much ado. If you go that route, try to get your statement out to members and relevant media contacts before the hearing. The most persuasive message in the world does not work if no one receives it.

Whether you are testifying in person or submitting a written statement, realize that members can only absorb so much information in a hearing. Thus, hone your oral testimony and written statement to a few important points that members can grasp and remember. State them in simple language and arrange them logically. If, for some reason, you need to provide a committee with a lot of detail, leave that to the written statement.

Think about ways to give a human-interest angle to your argument. Explain why the issue matters to average people. Members are much more likely to understand and remember your point if you tie it to an individual's story. Finally, if at all possible, speak your remarks conversationally rather than reading them. Nothing loses everyone's interest faster than a statement read aloud in a dull monotone.

Sometimes an organization should avoid a congressional hearing altogether. One such time is when it has engaged in indefensible conduct. You cannot defend the indefensible and you should not try. Another is when you believe your witness is going to lie. It does happen from time to time, and it should be avoided at all costs. Lying to Congress is a crime. It is much worse to suffer a criminal conviction than to suffer the wrath of members and staff.[17]

---

17. For more information on congressional hearings, see §§ 10.57–10.70 in *Lobbying and Advocacy* and § 8.40 and § 10.70 in *Congressional Deskbook*.

Chapter 37

The Markup

Committees recommend proposed legislation to their respective chambers through a process called a markup. In a markup, a committee formally meets to discuss, amend, and vote on a piece of legislation. The mechanics of how a markup works are set forth in Appendix E.

The chair determines when a committee will mark up a bill. Committee rules vary, but generally speaking, they allow a markup after a day or two's formal notice. However, on many bills, the chair will give informal notice well in advance.

As a markup of your bill approaches, you want to communicate regularly with the staff for the member who will champion your cause in the markup as well as the staffs of the chair and ranking member. You, your allies, and your champion should share all your intelligence with one another. All of you want to avoid any surprises. You should also work with your allies to provide those members who are helping you with anything they may need.

When the chair schedules a markup, a quorum—usually half the committee's members—must show up before the committee can vote on the bill. If there is no quorum, there is no markup. Depending on the committee, just getting a quorum can be a challenge. If you support the bill, you want to give the chair as much assistance as you can by urging members to show up. Likewise, if you oppose the bill, you may want to ask members to stay away if they cannot vote with you.

As best you can, you need to find out where your problems lie among the members of the committee and try to address these problems. Remember that for many members, the notice of the markup may force them to focus on the bill for the first time. They may not have previously known that it was coming up for consideration. Thus, you may have only a short time to educate them or their staffs about your point of view. It is a good idea to call staff for all members of a committee as soon as possible after a formal markup notice goes out. Be careful not to jump the gun before a formal notice goes out unless you have the chair's permission to tell other members when a bill will be marked up.

Most members are likely to follow the position of their party leader, either the chair or the ranking member, if they do not have some reason to do otherwise. If that chair or ranking member agrees with you, then you benefit. However, if they do not, then you need to get before the member or the staff as soon as you can and give them a reason to vote for your position.

Your champion, the chair, and the ranking member will usually have an idea of how they expect a markup to go. It may be that the bill goes on a voice vote with no amendments, it may involve a specific set of amendments, or it may be an unscripted free-for-all. You can best help your own position by listening closely to what members are planning and giving them your best input on the planned strategy. Ultimately, however, the members determine the course of the markup.

Finally, your work does not end when a markup begins. Although the members may have the outlines of a strategy going into a markup, these meetings are often "fly by the seat of the pants" affairs. Not every member may be aware of, or agree with, the strategy of the leaders, and they may feel free to deviate from it. If a bill is important to you, you need to have representatives in the room to speak for you. Often, deals are worked out and amendments are drafted while a markup is going on. Committee chairs may even pause a markup to confer with interested parties. In addition, markups are often interrupted by floor votes and other events that may give you a chance to talk to members about what is going in the markup. Make use of that opportunity if you need it.

After the markup, the committee staff writes a report on the bill that becomes publicly available. Committee reports can become important statements of legislative history later if the bill has difficult issues of interpretation that will come before the courts. Thus, if there are such issues, you want to provide as much input as the committee staff will allow on how the courts should interpret those questions. Those who voted against a bill can also file their own views as part of the report. If you are opposed to a bill, you should try to get those members to file views that give your reasons for opposing the legislation.

Woody Allen said "Showing up is eighty percent of life." That is certainly true in a markup. Members can only vote with you if they know your position. So show up, work hard, and reap the benefits.[18]

---

18. For more information on committee markups, see § 8.50 in *Congressional Deskbook.*

Chapter 38

Floor Consideration

Once your bill gets out of committee, you face a new challenge. Many bills get that far, but never make it to the floor. The majority party leaders decide if and when a bill will come to the floor. They have to mediate among many competing interests, and they have a limited amount of time to spend. Out of all the possibilities, you will have to convince them that your bill merits the use of the precious resource of floor time.

In making that decision, they are going to look beyond a good policy rationale and see whether the bill falls into one of several general categories. The first is that the bill has relatively little controversy and therefore will not create a difficult vote for any members. Many relatively minor bills will fall into this category. The second is that the bill creates good votes for the majority party while creating difficult votes for the minority party. Third, on some bills, public opinion will simply require the bill's consideration irrespective of the consequences. For example, every year, the majority party leaders must bring up appropriations bills to fund the government's operations. Likewise, the stimulus package passed in early 2009 fell into this category.

From your earliest thinking about positioning, you need to think about how to make the case for floor time for your bill. Once your bill begins to get momentum in committee, you will want to start working with the party leaders to lay the groundwork for floor consideration. First, let them know your bill exists and that you care about it. Unless your bill attracts broad public attention, they may not know anything about it. Second, educate them about what the bill does and why it is important. If the bill has any controversy at all, you will want to start this effort earlier rather than later.

If you succeed in convincing the leaders to bring up your bill, they will usually let you know that and give you a general sense of the time frame. Then your whole perspective changes. You are dealing with a much larger group of members who know much less about your bill than you were when it was in committee. Fortunately, however, the universe of possible amendments that you are going to have to deal with is usually much smaller.

Assuming you favor the bill, as soon as it gets out of committee, start getting your message out to other members of the chamber who may know little about it. Even if it will be a while before the bill gets to the floor, you need to start educating those who may be with you when it does come up. That can take some time, and you want to start early.

Floor amendment procedures differ substantially in the House and the Senate. For major bills, the House usually passes a "rule" that sets forth the terms of debate and what amendments members may offer. The House Rules Committee gives members an opportunity to submit proposed amendments before fashioning the rule. Usually, it will hold a hearing at which members testify about the amendments that they have submitted. After the hearing, the committee formally sets the terms of the rule and sends it to the full House.

As a practical matter, the majority party leaders in the House dictate the result in the Rules Committee particularly for the more important bills and amendments. If you are trying to get an amendment into or out of the rule, your best bet is to work with the Speaker, the Majority Leader, and the Rules Committee chair. If your issue is more peripheral, other members of the Rules Committee may be able to help, but generally they are expected to toe the line the leaders set down.

The rule is usually published the day before the House considers the bill. When the bill comes up the next day, the House must first adopt the rule. In most cases, there is one hour of debate on the rule and it is simply an extension of the debate on the bill itself. The vote on a rule

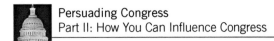
is almost always a straight party line vote although in rare instances, the minority's position may attract enough members of the majority party to threaten the rule's passage. In that case, the bill is likely to be pulled before the vote takes place.

Because rules are reported the day before floor consideration, you usually have twenty-four hours to make House members aware of your position on the amendments. Fortunately, with email, you can get this information out quickly. It may be the case that you do not care about most of the amendments. If so, you do not need to communicate that. If an amendment is crucial to your cause, then you may have to mount a full scale lobbying effort. You should try to reach as many members as possible, but word usually spreads fast when there is real controversy.

In the Senate, amendments are usually not limited in number or subject unless all senators agree (known as "unanimous consent"). Thus, you can almost always get a topic addressed in the Senate as long as you have one friendly senator who is willing to offer an amendment on any bill that may be under consideration.

However, on most bills, the leaders reach some agreement to limit amendments. If it looks like an agreement is going to happen, you want to get your input on the shape of the agreement to the party leaders as early as possible. If you are not happy with the shape of the proposed agreement to limit amendments, you need to let friendly senators know that you want them to object to the proposed agreement.

If you oppose a bill in either chamber, you first want to fight its ever coming up. On that front, your two principal tools are delay and controversy. Use any plausible excuse to delay consideration as long as possible. Then argue to the leaders that consideration will cause difficult votes for the members of their party. Remember that the leaders depend on the goodwill of the members of their party to remain in their positions and they do not want to create a lot of difficult political situations for them in their districts. That is the fastest way for them to lose their jobs.

If the bill is definitely coming up, then you want to give your champions ideas for amendments that will create tough votes for the proponents. That is your best way to kill the bill or slow its consideration. If you just need a small change to the bill to make it acceptable, then let the leaders know that and try to get someone to offer your tweak as an amendment.

The keys to floor consideration are knowledge and communication. You can only know what is going on if you stay in close touch with the party leaders, the chair, the ranking member, your champion, and your allies. Other members can only do what you want them to do if you tell them what it is.[19]

---

19. For more information on House and Senate floor consideration, see §§ 8.70–8.250 in *Congressional Deskbook*.

Chapter 39

The Conference

The rules restrict much of what goes on in Congress. But when the two chambers pass differing versions of a bill and appoint members to a conference committee to resolve those differences, it is the wild, wild West. Conference committees have only two significant rules: they must have one public meeting and a majority of the members of the conference committee from each chamber must sign the final product. Other than that, pretty much anything goes. The conference committee can insert all sorts of things into the bill that were not in either chamber's version.

Once a conference committee reports back to the chambers, the chambers generally cannot amend the committee's final product. For that reason, members love to get to conference. It is a great way to get things done that they could not get done in the light of day. Indeed, if you are pushing something that is a good idea, but cannot pass in an open vote, then a conference is your best, and probably only, chance for success.

The key to a conference is again to stick close to the party leaders and the chairs and ranking members of the respective committees. They will control what goes into the final product of the conference. If they are on your side, there is not much anyone else can do about it so long as they keep the overall product acceptable to a majority.

They will generally try to tightly control information about what is actually going in to a bill to prevent people from attacking it. If possible, they will try to move quickly. In that situation, you need as many friends among the members and staff working on the conference as you can. You would like to trust everybody, but you cannot always.

Members want to get as much of what they want into the bill as they can while keeping it acceptable to a majority of both chambers. They may make tradeoffs that you do not like for the benefit of getting the overall deal done, and you may get left out in the cold. Conference is a time of great danger and great opportunity. Be wary.[20]

---

20. For more information on how House and Senate bills are reconciled, see §§ 8.260–8.283 of *Congressional Deskbook*.

Chapter 40

Crisis

A Chinese proverb says: "In every crisis there is opportunity." Nowhere is that more true than in a legislature.

When the public perceives a crisis, legislators want to do something. It does not matter that doing nothing may be a far better response to the crisis. It does not matter that the "something" will have little effect on the crisis or will make it worse. If the public is astir, legislators are going to legislate.

Crisis frequently means that whatever legislation the leadership puts on the floor will pass regardless of the merits. The financial bailout legislation that Congress enacted in the fall of 2008 and the stimulus package enacted in early 2009 are prime examples. Many members had serious misgivings about these bills, but they passed anyway with only minimal debate and vetting.

That type of situation creates great opportunity for the agile leader of an organization. If your idea relates to the crisis in any way, you may be able to get it attached to the moving legislative vehicle. If you have any colorable claim that your idea could actually contribute to solving the problem, all the better.

The trick is getting it attached to the moving vehicle. It is best if your idea has hung around for a while and has had some vetting. At the beginning of a crisis, staffers frequently gather up all the ideas that have resided on their plate for the last several years and throw them into the bill as the solution to the crisis. Such bills usually receive less than full process. If you can get your idea in the first draft, you may get it enacted with little additional effort.

Generally speaking, the chairs of the relevant committees and the party leaders control what goes into these bills. Rank-and-file members have relatively little say. They are usually faced with an up-or-down vote on the whole package without any chance for amendment. In fact, they are often asked to vote with little chance to even read the bill.

Your fate in these moments rests in the hands of the chairs and the party leaders. That is why it is so important to build long-term relationships with them. When a crisis happens, everyone in the world will be calling them trying to get their idea into the bill. You want them to return your call at that moment, and you want them to put your idea in the bill.

By the same token, if your opponent is trying to get his idea into the bill, you may not even know it until it is too late. Again, the chairs and the party leaders hold all the cards. If you have built a relationship with them, you have a much better chance of getting a call from them if something you do not like is being considered for inclusion.

A crisis offers great opportunity and great danger. Politics is a long-term game, and the winners are those who build long-term relationships.

G. Long-Term Considerations

Summary of Chapters 41–44

- Getting anything passed in Congress is a cumbersome process. If you have a short time frame, think through whether there is some other way to solve your problem before going to Congress for a legislative solution. If you decide to go to Congress, have a realistic attitude about how quickly Congress can act. (*Chapter 41*)

- The relative intensity of the parties can affect Congress greatly. If one side feels much more strongly than the other, it may win even though it is much smaller than the other. (*Chapter 42*)

- If you are going to get in the lobbying game, you must be willing to take political risk. Have the courage to act to resolve issues rather than spend money fighting the same battles over and over. (*Chapter 43*)

- For a variety of reasons, members and staff will inevitably disappoint you from time to time. Understand that this is a normal part of the process. Do not take it personally and do not to let it stand in the way of an otherwise productive relationship. (*Chapter 44*)

Chapter 41

Patience

Congress is not a miracle machine. It is large, clunky, and slow. Getting things done there is cumbersome. The legislative process is slow by design; only in rare circumstances does Congress pass laws quickly. If your timeline is short, consider whether you can solve your problem in any other way before trying to get a law passed.

If your problem can only be solved by passing a law, enter the process understanding that it will take a while. Many leaders frequently have completely unrealistic expectations on this score. They think that they can identify a problem, explain the solution, and have Congress enact that solution in a couple of weeks. It does not work that way. If you expect that, you will find yourself banging your head against the wall in frustration.

Passing complicated laws that involve a lot of conflicting interests frequently takes several Congresses. If you are involved in such a process, you have to stay with it. You will have ups and downs, stops and starts, victories and losses. You must remember that it is a marathon, not a sprint.

Expressing frustration to members and staff about how slow the process is accomplishes little and may in fact alienate your potential supporters. You can rest assured that they are equally frustrated, but they must work within the system as it is, not as they wish it to be. You should always express your desire to get the best product possible for their constituents and ask what you can do to move the process forward. Better yet, to the extent that you can, create reasons for members to benefit from moving forward.

Chapter 42

Intensity

L obbyists sometimes talk about an intensity issue. What they mean is that one side cares much more deeply about the issue than the other side. Thus, the intense desires of that side may preclude any movement on the issue.

This is common in business issues. It usually occurs when a small group of people or companies benefit enormously from an existing law or program. Typically, a much larger number of people bear the cost of that law or program, but they do so in tiny increments.

The beneficiaries know about the law or program, follow it closely, and are prepared to fight to the death to preserve it. On the other hand, those paying for it are usually unaware of it. Even if they are aware, the small incremental cost they pay gives them little incentive to fight against it. Because of this imbalance, policies that clearly do not serve the public as a whole can stay on the books for years even though everyone knows they should be repealed.

If intensity can save bad policies, it can also help you. You are always better off if those on your side of an issue feel more intensely about it than those on the other side. Congress responds to pressure. When people feel intensely about an issue, they put the pressure on Congress.

Intensity is to a large extent organic. People feel the way they feel and they act accordingly. However, you can arouse intensity in some situations by showing people that the issue matters to them or someone they care about. Intensity can also sometimes occur because of some procedural unfairness.

Human behavior is too complex to give much general advice about what will stir someone's intensity. When you feel that something should stir your allies' intensity, emphasize that aspect. However, to work, intensity must be real—not faked. If you try to get people to fake it, that will fail.

Understanding the intensity of your opponents can also help you decide what is possible. If you face a classic intensity issue situation, think long and hard before you invest your money in trying to change the situation. Make sure your allies are prepared to fight before you start that war. By the same token, if your likely opponents are not very intense, you may be able to slip your proposal through with relatively little controversy.

The relative intensity of the various players can be hard to discern, but it should always enter into your congressional calculations.

Chapter 43

Courage

Nothing ventured, nothing gained—this is as true in the legislative market of Capitol Hill as it is in economic markets. If you are not willing to take at least some reasonable political risk, do not waste your time putting money into lobbying. Save your money, sit on the sidelines, and accept the consequences.

Unfortunately, many organizations spend their money, get in the game nominally, and then take no risks. Not surprisingly, they get the exact same results as those who do not spend their money and do not pretend to be in the game.

This does not mean that you should act rashly or foolishly. But it does mean that when opportunity arises, you must seize the day. For example, an excellent witness can turn the tide of a legislative debate at a committee hearing. But if an organization will not risk having that witness testify, it will not get that reward. Far too often, political opportunity comes toward an organization, it mulls the opportunity over slowly, and the opportunity passes by. A week or two later, the organization pops its head up and asks if it can still play, but by that time it is too late. The opportunity is well down the road and the organization cannot recapture it.

One reason that this happens is that, unfortunately, many organizations structure their lobbying operations so that their representatives cannot get an answer in time to act effectively. Your person on the ground on Capitol Hill must be able to get direction when needed—not two weeks later. Set up your operation in any way that suits your needs, but ensure that your person on the ground can get a quick answer.

You must also create an environment in which your lobbyists are not paralyzed. Too often, organizations structure their lobbying teams so that the only strong incentive the lobbyists have is to avoid making mistakes. They get little reward for moving things forward in the face of any perceived risk. In that situation, their bias is always for inaction. Nothing happens, and opportunities for success continually slip by. If you are not going to give your lobbyists the freedom to make a few mistakes, save your money. You are not going to get any value from lobbyists who spend all their time trying to preserve their jobs by not doing anything useful. Understand also that it is difficult for lobbyists to quantify their value in dollar terms. Accept that and do not create perverse incentives by insisting that they show their value that way.

In the same vein, you have no doubt heard the admonition: do not let the perfect be the enemy of the good. Quite often, an organization can get an acceptable bill passed, but it holds out for something better that may or may not come later. Opportunities to enact legislation only come around every so often. When you have the chance to take a bird in the hand, weigh the pros and cons carefully. Do not reject the bird simply because: (1) you think it is possible you will get more later; (2) you would like more; (3) you think justice requires that you get more; or (4) you cannot stand to see your adversaries get anything at all. Think through whether you can live with what you have before you and whether you are ever likely to get anything more. Predictions in this arena are necessarily uncertain for a multitude of reasons, and you will make mistakes. The important point is that you should always remember that good enough may be all you need and all you will ever get.

For the same reason, do not fear compromise. Some people worry that compromise will diminish their stature or mark them as weak. In fact, legislative accomplishment springs from it. Too often, an organization refuses to negotiate at all when a perfectly suitable compromise is at hand for all parties. Or having agreed to sit together with adversaries to negotiate, an organization simply sits and spins its wheels. If you are going to come to the table, negotiate and do not be afraid to ask for what you need. If you have no intention of negotiating, then tell everyone that truthfully and let the chips fall where they may.

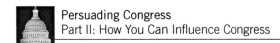

Lobbyists often joke about sending their children to college on one big bill that comes up Congress after Congress. It is a great deal for them, but not for you. Do not let yourself be the butt of that joke. If a bill affects you, have the courage to act to resolve the issue and avoid spending more and more money fighting the same old battles year after year.

Chapter 44

Understanding

N o matter how close you are to a particular member of Congress or staffer, that person will inevitably disappoint you from time to time. For a myriad of reasons that have nothing to do with you, the person will not always do what you want them to do, even though from your perspective it seems that they should want to do it. Political winds shift frequently, and politicians must shift with them to survive.

Accept this as a normal part of the process and do not take it personally. Success in Congress depends on long-term relationships. If you work hard at building and maintaining long-term relationships, you are going to succeed more often than if you do not have those relationships. Do not let one disappointing incident spoil an otherwise productive relationship.

When disappointments occur, you may feel that the person owed you something. You may well be right. Most members and staffers get that dynamic and they will be looking for an opportunity to make it up to you later. Thus, it is best never to mention this, but simply leave it unspoken. When you see the opportunity for them to make it up, make them aware of it, but do not tell them that they owe you one. If they are any good, they will figure it out.

Long-term relationships also sustain the member's survival. For that reason, you do not have to be a doormat for a member. If you are repeatedly disappointed or abused by a member, think about quietly withdrawing from that relationship and finding others. Most members know that they need you as much as you need them, but there are always some who do not.

Chapter 45

Conclusion

Having read this book, you should understand more about where members are coming from, what drives them, how to behave appropriately around them, and when to give them a pass. And you should understand that in the legislative arena, there are no permanent victories and no permanent defeats. Make wise choices about what is realistic, but having committed your organization to seeking something from Congress, do not give up. Patience, discipline, and quality ideas yield the best results over the long run.

Appendices

Appendix A
The Constitutional Basics

The Founding Fathers created Congress during the Constitutional Convention in 1787. They set forth the organizational outlines of Congress in Article I of the Constitution. Those outlines have changed little since then.

Congress consists of two, co-equal chambers, the House of Representatives and the Senate. The House consists of 435 Representatives (also commonly referred to as "members of Congress" or "congressmen") who are elected from the states for two-year terms. The District of Columbia and several of the territories send delegates to Congress—those delegates can vote in committees, but not in the full House.

After every ten-year census, representatives are apportioned among the states according to their population. The Constitution does not require the states to elect their representatives from districts, but a statute passed by Congress in 1967 requires election of representatives from single-member districts. Pub. L. No. 90-196; 2 U.S.C. § 2c. A few small states get only one representative and that person is elected statewide. The populations of the districts within a state must have approximately the same population, but they vary slightly from state to state. Currently, each congressional district contains approximately 600,000 to 700,000 people.

Senators were originally elected by the legislatures of their state. As a result of the 17th Amendment ratified in 1913, senators are now directly elected by the people of their states. Each state has two senators irrespective of population. Thus, the size of the constituencies that senators represent varies greatly depending on the population of their states. Nonetheless, each senator has an equal vote in the Senate's deliberations. Senators are elected for six-year terms.

A bill only becomes a law if both the House and the Senate pass it in exactly the same form. A majority of the members of each chamber must vote for the bill. The bill is then presented to the president. In most cases, the president signs the bill and it becomes law with his signature. Occasionally, the president will veto the bill. In that case, the bill is sent back to Congress and it votes again. To override the veto, two-thirds of each chamber must vote in favor of the bill. If they do, it becomes law over the president's objection.

Within these broad parameters, each chamber may adopt its own rules of procedure. The rules of the House and the Senate differ significantly.

A Congress lasts for two years. Each year within the Congress is known as a session. Thus, 2009 was the First Session of the 111th Congress, and 2010 was the Second Session. At the end of a Congress, all legislative activity in that Congress dies. Bills that have not made it to the president by the end of a Congress must start over again from the beginning in the next Congress.

You should also keep in mind that the two chambers also have certain non-legislative powers, like oversight of executive agencies and the confirmation of executive nominees, that may sometimes affect what is happening in the legislative arena.

The Founders designed this system to fail in most instances, and that is what it does. That, of course, assumes that you define success as passing laws. In general, Congress can only pass laws when a broad public consensus supports them.

A "Pocket Constitution" is available at no charge from TheCapitol. Net; see *<TCNConst.com>*.

Appendix B
Tips on Hiring a Lobbyist

- **Ask around.** Ask other people in your area which lobbyists they have used. If you have an in-house government affairs person, ask that person which lobbyists are good.

- **Meet before you hire.** A lobbyist's success or failure depends heavily on how people react to him or her as a person. Meet with the lobbyist before you hire him or her and see if the reaction that you have is the one that you want people to have about your company. Remember the lobbyist becomes the face of your company to the people he or she contacts. If you feel the lobbyist is sleazy, then others will probably feel that way.

- **Find one you like.** If you have a problem that requires hiring a lobbyist, then you are probably going to be spending some time with that person. Find one whose personality you like. In addition, the lobbying game depends a lot on personal relationships. Thus, in general, a lobbyist who has a good personality is going to succeed more often than one who does not.

- **Look for realism.** One of the most important things that a lobbyist can do for you is to give you a realistic assessment of your chances. If a lobbyist tells you this is going to be easy, look for someone else.

- **Look for availability.** A lobbyist does not do you much good if you cannot get in touch with him or her. You are paying good money for the services. You should be able to get your lobbyist on the phone or meet with him or her within a reasonable time.

- **Look for reasonable fees.** Most lobbying is done on a retainer basis, which tends to work out well for both sides. The amount of work tends to vary widely from month to month, depending on the circumstances. Retainers help to even things out for both sides. Many lobbying retainers run anywhere from $5,000 to $30,000 a month, depending on the amount of work expected.

- **Beware of big names.** Big-name lobbyists can be very effective— if they have time to devote to your problem. However, many of them have so many clients that they have little personal time to devote to your problem. They are also going to cost you more than a typical lobbyist. Think through whether it is worthwhile to pay more for less of their time.

- **Beware of guarantees.** What happens in Congress turns on many forces that are beyond any one person's control. If any lobbyist tells you that they can guarantee you a particular result, be wary. They cannot, and that assertion should make you question everything else that they say.

- **Beware of corner-cutters.** Make sure that your lobbyist complies fully with all legal and ethical restrictions. If a lobbyist starts to suggest ways to cut corners on those things, it is probably time to look for another lobbyist. You have enough problems— you do not need a lobbyist who creates more for you.

- **Keep the contract to no more than one year.** Most lobbying contracts are for no more than one year. Generally speaking, they contain a provision that says you can end the relationship whenever you want, but most businesses simply do not renew them at the end of the year if they are not satisfied. Having frequent renewals ensures that you get good service.

Appendix C

The Roles of Party Leaders

In the House, the majority party elects the Speaker of the House, the majority leader, the majority whip, the party conference chair, and the head of the party's campaign committee.[21] The minority party chooses the minority leader, the minority whip, the party conference chair, and the head of the party's campaign committee.

In the Senate, the offices are similar except that there is no Speaker. Rather, the vice president of the United States serves as the president of the Senate, however, the only power of the vice president in that capacity is to cast a tie-breaking vote.[22]

In the House, the Speaker is the overall leader of the majority party. She sets the policy direction of the party and has the most influence in party decisions like what committee assignments members of her party will get and what bills to bring to the floor. The majority leader is her second in command. He assists her in all these functions, but is more involved in the daily scheduling and jousting on the floor. The majority whip has the primary responsibility for rounding up votes for party positions.

The conference chair works to communicate an overall message to the press and the public and to ensure that members are informed of that message. The campaign committee chairman heads the party's efforts to advance its cause in the next election.

The minority leaders have basically the same functions for their party except that the minority leader combines the functions of the Speaker and the majority leader for the minority party. In other words, the minority leader is both the overall leader of the party and the floor manager for the minority.

---

21. The Speaker theoretically presides over the debate in the House, but that rarely happens in practice. Members of the majority party take turns presiding, usually for an hour at the time.

22. In practice, the vice president rarely presides in the Senate except during a close vote or a ceremonial occasion. Like the House, members of the majority party take turns presiding over the Senate. The most senior member of the majority party is the president pro tempore, but this is a largely ceremonial office.

In the Senate, the functions of the various leaders are much the same as they are in the House. The only exception is that the majority leader combines the functions of the Speaker and the majority leader of the House.[23]

---

23. For more information about party leadership, see §§ 7.40–7.44 of *Congressional Deskbook*.

House Leadership Structure, 111th Congress

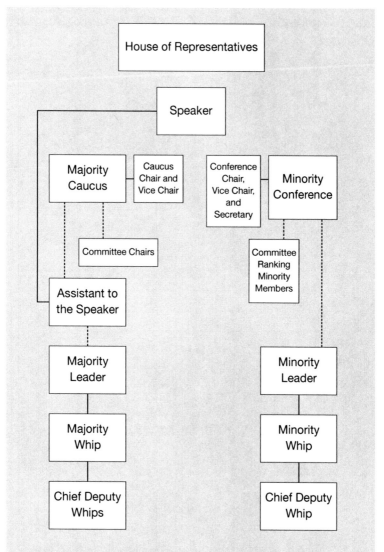

Solid lines indicate a direct relationship in terms of shared responsibilities.
Dashed lines indicate a less formal relationship.

For the current House leadership, see TheCapitol.Net web page <*www.CongressLeaders.com*>.

This chart is reproduced from § 7.42 of the *Congressional Deskbook*, by Michael Koempel and Judy Schneider. Copyright © 2007 by TheCapitol.Net. All Rights Reserved. <*www.thecapitol.net*>

Senate Leadership Structure, 111th Congress

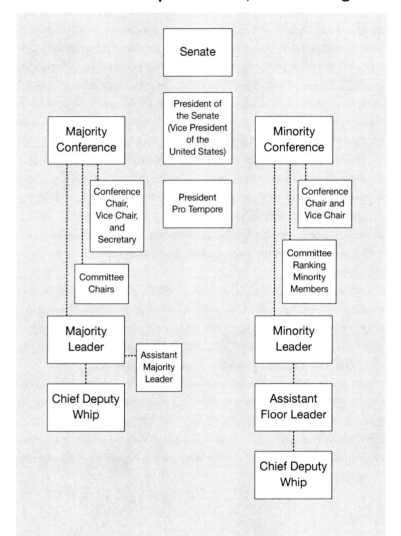

Solid lines indicate a direct relationship in terms of shared responsibilities.
Dashed lines indicate a less formal relationship.

For the current Senate leadership, see TheCapitol.Net web page <www.CongressLeaders.com>.

This chart is reproduced from § 7.44 of the *Congressional Deskbook*, by Michael Koempel and Judy Schneider. Copyright © 2007 by TheCapitol.Net. All Rights Reserved. <www.thecapitol.net>

Appendix D
How a Hearing Works

Exact rules and practices vary from one committee to another, but the general outlines of a hearing are much the same for all committees. At a hearing, the chairman of the committee invites a number of witnesses to testify. This is usually done in consultation with the ranking member of the committee. In some cases, the minority may be allowed to choose a certain number of the witnesses. Most chairs call witnesses with a variety of views to give a broad overview of the issue.

The witnesses will prepare written statements and give them to the committee a day or two before the hearing. Then on the day of the hearing, they orally present an abbreviated version of their testimony. Most committees limit these oral statements to five minutes. The witnesses generally appear on panels of several witnesses and the committee may have one or more panels, but usually there are no more than three panels.

When a hearing opens, the chair will call it to order and give an opening statement in which the chair sets the stage for the hearing and gives his position on the issue if he has one. Then the ranking member gives a statement that states his position if he has one. Some committees allow other members to make opening statements as well.

After the opening statements, each witness on the panel is allowed to make an oral statement. After all witnesses on the panel have given their oral statement, each member of the committee has an allotted time, usually five minutes, to ask questions of the witnesses on the panel. Enforcement of the time limit varies from committee to committee.

Appendix E
How a Markup Works

Similar to hearings, committees have slightly different rules and practices about how they conduct markups, but the general pattern is the same for all. The chair decides when a bill will be marked up and gives whatever notice the rules require—usually a day or two. Some committees require that members file their amendments in advance, and some do not.

When the noticed time arrives, the chair calls up the bill. The chair makes a short statement on the bill and then allows the ranking member to do the same. These are usually five minutes long. Some committees allow other members to make opening statements as well.

Once these statements are made, the chair asks if any members want to offer any amendments to the bill. Members then seek recognition from the chair and offer their amendments. Once a member offers an amendment, that member gives a brief statement explaining it. The proponents of the bill may accept it in which case it is usually adopted by a voice vote of the committee. Or they may contest it in which case a member opposed to the amendment will give a statement explaining why the member opposes it. Other members may join the debate after that. When all members have had their say, the chair calls a vote and the amendment is either adopted or it is not. Any member may request a recorded vote in which case the clerk calls the members' names individually and records their votes.

Sometimes, members may offer amendments simply to get someone's attention. They may be seeking a concession of some sort—usually a commitment to work on the issue further before the bill comes up on the floor. Or they may simply want to make a point without pushing the issue to a vote. In those cases, they may withdraw the amendment before it is voted on.

When the chair determines that all members have had a chance to offer all of their amendments, he calls for a vote on the bill as the committee has amended it. As with amendment votes, any member may request a recorded vote. After the vote, the chair moves on to the next bill on the agenda and the process goes forward again. Typically, a committee will vote on several bills during any single markup.[24]

---

24. For more information on committee markups, see § 8.50 of *Congressional Deskbook*.

Index

Breinigsville, PA USA
23 March 2010
234756BV00005B/1/P

9 781587 331640